FARMERS, FORESTS AND FUEL

Farmers, Forests and Fuel

Towards a new biomass energy strategy for Sri Lanka

MICK HOWES
with
Pandula Endagama

INTERMEDIATE TECHNOLOGY PUBLICATIONS 1995

Published by Intermediate Technology Publications
103/105 Southampton Row London WCIB 4HH, UK

ISBN 1 85339 089 5

A CIP catalogue record for this book is available
from the British Library

Typeset by J&L Composition Ltd, Filey, North Yorkshire
Printed in UK by BPC Wheatons

Contents

Maps

Figures

Acknowledgements

A large number of people have helped in the preparation of this book. Andrew Barnett, Martin Greeley, Gerald Leach and Mick Moore all provided guidance in the initial stages, when the research was being planned. Bill Gauld carried out the preliminary literature review and made an important contribution to the first fieldwork study.

In Sri Lanka, H. Amararatna, K.H. Liyanage, Y.A.V.S. Perera and R.K.P.A. Wickramasuriya worked hard to gather and analyse the primary data upon which the greater part of the report is based.

Valuable advice and assistance were also received from: Lamasena and Steve Raggett of Sarvodaya; Madugoda and Gary Shea of the Community Forestry Project; Professor Rajaguru and Dr Ajith Perera of Peradeniya University; P.S. Ramakrishnan of the Ministry of Plan Implementation; Wickrama of the Hambantota IRDP; G.B.A. Fernando and R.M. Amarasekera of the Ceylon Electricity Board; D. Gamage of ARTI; J.M. Eastwood of the British High Commission; K. Dayananda and Dr R. Vivekanandan of the Forest Department; and Dr F.R. Senananayake of the Neosynthesis Research Centre.

We are grateful to Kate Clarke and Pete Young of ITDG and to David Hall of King's College, London for their comments on earlier drafts of the report, and to Amanda Davey for preparing the maps (redrawn for this book by Richard Inglis).

Finally, we would like to express our gratitude to the Agrarian Research and Training Centre in Colombo for providing an institutional base during our fieldwork, and to ESCOR for their financial support.

The views expressed are our own and do not necessarily reflect those of the funding agency. We are solely responsible for any errors or omissions.

List of acronyms

ADB	Asian Development Bank
AGA	Assistant Government Agent
ARTI	Agrarian Research and Training Institute
CEB	Ceylon Electricity Board
CFP	Community Forestry Project
DCO	District Co-ordinating Officer
ECT	Energy Co-ordinating Team
EDMAC	Energy Demand Management and Conservation Committee
EPPAN	Energy Planning and Policy Analysis Committee
FD	Forestry Department
FMP	Forestry Master Plan
IRDP	Integrated Rural Development Project
ITD	Intermediate Technology Development Group
JEDB	Janata Estates Development Board
LDO	Land Development Ordinance
MPE	Ministry of Power and Energy
NFCP	National Fuelwood Conservation Programme
NARESA	Natural Resources, Science and Energy Authority
NRSEC	New and Renewable Sources of Energy Committee
SLFP	Sri Lanka Freedom Party
UNDP	United Nations Development Programme
UNP	United National Party
WFP	World Food Programme

SECTION I
BACKGROUND

1. The 'Other Energy Crisis' and its critics

The problem

In the mid-1970s, as the relatively wealthy minority of the world's population sought to come to terms with the first round of oil price increases, it was suggested that the poor were confronted by an equally serious, but hitherto unrecognized, energy problem of their own. Labelled 'The Other Energy Crisis', this was said to take the form of growing shortages of the biomass fuels which they had traditionally used for cooking, and a range of other subsistence and market-oriented activities[1].

The issue soon became linked to others which were themselves attracting growing international attention at the time, and rapidly assumed a prominent position on the agenda of the major development agencies. Within a few years, a large number of initiatives had been set in motion, covering all major geographical regions of the Third World.

But even as this process was gathering momentum, dissenting voices began to be heard; arguing that the extent and nature of this 'crisis' had been incorrectly perceived, and that the solutions which were being advocated were accordingly flawed.

This book explores the phenomenon of the 'other energy crisis' in the context of Sri Lanka: a country which was believed to be in fuel deficit, and one where ameliorative actions – typical of those attempted in many other places – have been pursued. At one level, *Farmers, Forests and Fuel* may therefore be seen as a test case, through which the merits of the arguments advanced internationally by the

3

proponents and the critics of the notion of crisis can be assessed.

It is not, however, only about energy; for the immediate issue of energy policy poses more fundamental questions about how, and by whom, rural development 'problems' are currently defined; about the more general consequences of these decision-making structures; and about the possibility of modified forms of interaction between those who presently make decisions, and those who must take them.

Formative influences

The notion of the 'Other Energy Crisis' derives from Eckholm's 1975 paper of the same name, although it is important to distinguish between his formulation of the problem, and the dominant construction which has subsequently been placed upon it.[2] It was also Eckholm who pointed to the possible connection between declining fuel availability, deforestation and environmental degradation, thus helping the original problem to achieve greater prominence than might otherwise have been the case.[3] The sense of crisis, and the perceived need for action on a substantial scale, drew further strength from the growing attention commanded by questions of gender during the 1970s, and by the recognition that it was likely that women would be affected first and most severely where shortages of fuel arose.[4] This cocktail of ideas quickly began to attract attention in international development circles, and as the decade drew to a close, the UN Food and Agriculture Organization (FAO) decided to undertake a study which would help to indicate the extent of the problem.[5]

When the findings were presented in 1981, they appeared to provide ample confirmation of the fears which had been expressed. Some 1.4 billion people were found to be suffering from either deficit or from 'acute fuelwood shortage' and it was predicted that their number could double by the end of the century. The great majority of those affected were thought to be located in rural areas. This study and the conclusions at which it arrived were probably the most important single influence upon what followed.

Even before the FAO had completed its work, many initiatives had been launched. Domestic cooking stove programmes were established in many countries, with the

4

expectation that substantial fuel savings could be achieved through improvements in the efficiency with which biomass was converted.[6] At the same time, an even larger movement was underway to promote new forms of forestry, which could satisfy the long-term need for alternative sources of energy supply.[7] By 1984, a sum not far short of a billion dollars had been spent in pursuit of these objectives.

Key features of the response

The approaches adopted in different countries tended, with rather few exceptions, to be based upon five related assumptions. These were that:

o rural people were either unaware of the extent of the problem with which they were confronted, or were unable to solve it for themselves;

o the problem was one of the physical availability of fuel, and could therefore be solved by purely technical means;

o the nature of the crisis was essentially the same, irrespective of where it arose and could therefore be dealt with through the introduction of a broadly uniform package of measures;

o a classic 'blueprint' approach, with centrally set targets, to be achieved within specified periods of time, represented the best way of proceeding;

o fuel shortages forced people to cut down trees, which, in turn, caused environmental damage; measures which saved fuel or created alternative sources of supply would therefore simultaneously provide environmental protection.

The critics

As increasing numbers of initiatives of this type were taken, criticisms began to emerge. Some concerned the way in which governments and donors had sought to address the issue. Others went so far as to suggest that there was no real crisis at all.

Whilst generally not disagreeing with Eckholm's basic proposition that substantial numbers of poor people might be encountering difficulty in satisfying their fuel needs,

5

critics have questioned the way in which the problem has subsequently been formulated. The points which have been raised may be grouped together into a small number of categories:

○ *Differing environments.* It has been suggested that the kinds and quantities of biomass fuel available to users are subject to large variations within a country. If this is correct, shortages are unlikely to be uniformly distributed, and interventions should therefore be geographically targeted.

○ *Biomass in context.* It has been argued that biomass fuels are seldom produced in isolation. They are normally obtained from trees or crops which simultaneously satisfy one or more other needs, some of which will generally be regarded as being more important than fuel itself. Viewed in this light, the availability of fuel becomes at least partially a function of the more general resource-allocation decisions being taken by those who control land, and cannot sensibly be discussed in isolation from this wider context. Where a shortage of fuel arises, in other words, we may well not simply be dealing with a clearly isolable question of energy crisis.

○ *Differences in access.* The third point builds upon the second. If biomass derives, in significant measure, from privately operated land, it has been reasoned that the effects of any shortage within a specific locality will not be evenly distributed. Rather, they will fall, to a disproportionate extent, upon the resource poor. From this perspective, shortages no longer appear as purely physical phenomena, amenable to solution by solely technical means, and instead they assume a socio-economic dimension.

○ *Indigenous responses.* It has been suggested that all fuel users, and rural people in particular, have a repertoire of potential responses at their disposal if they are confronted by shortages. From this, it has been proposed that, at the very least, one should be looking at the possibility of solutions arrived at by a process of interaction between indigenous and external expertise and that pure blueprint planning should be ruled out of court.

○ *Environmental impact.* A final line of attack, based

again upon a growing appreciation of the diversity of sources from which fuel is typically obtained, has been directed at the assumed linkages between fuel consumption, deforestation and environmental destruction.

The book in outline

The chapters which follow provide an opportunity to determine how far these criticisms, and the alternative approach which would appear to follow from them, are borne out by the Sri Lankan experience.

Chapter 2, which completes the introductory section, traces the evolution of energy policy-making in Sri Lanka from its origins in 1974, and sets a context within which to explore the more specific biomass-related interventions which are considered later in the book.

Section II comprises two further chapters. These review the proposition that it is unhelpful to think in terms of national biomass energy deficit, and describe a methodology which enables the extent of shortages to be disaggregated both by geographical location and socio-economic group. Chapter 3 draws exclusively upon secondary sources. Chapter 4 reports findings derived from a series of field studies conducted in various parts of Sri Lanka in 1987. An account of the methods employed and the locations covered appears in Appendix 1.

Section III describes the major biomass-related interventions with which the Government of Sri Lanka has been associated; assesses their overall effectiveness; and spells out their implications for different sets of people. Chapter 5 looks in detail at the Community Forestry Project (CFP), and Chapter 6 at the promotion of stoves under the National Fuelwood Conservation Programme (NFCP). Both utilize a combination of materials from the field studies and secondary sources.

The final section returns to the most general themes raised in the introduction, seeking to explain the outcomes of the interventions, to explore alternative solutions to Sri Lanka's biomass energy problems, and to sketch in some broader principles regarding the role which the state might most usefully perform when confronted by a rather complicated and highly differentiated rural economy.

Notes

1. The expression biomass energy will refer throughout this book to all parts of trees, and to all other vegetative matter used as fuel. Readers should be alerted to the fact that often expressions such as 'fuelwood' or 'firewood' are used when the actual reference ought to be to biomass as it is more widely defined here. This has contributed to the confusion about the relationship between fuel use and deforestation which is explored later.
2. Eckholm (1975).
3. Eckholm (1976).
4. Agarwal (1986).
5. FAO (1981).
6. Joseph (1983).
7. Foley and Bernard (1984).

2. Biomass in the evolution of Sri Lankan energy policy

The account of biomass in the evolution of Sri Lankan energy policy begins in the period immediately preceding the first round of oil price increases in 1973–4, and continues up until 1987, when the fieldwork part of our research was completed. Two broad phases are identified, the dividing line between them being marked by the second round of major price rises which occurred in 1978.

The initial round of oil price increases: 1974–8

The situation prior to 1974
In 1973, before oil prices were increased for the first time, Sri Lanka had no overall energy policy. Petroleum was administered by the State Petroleum Corporation, and electricity by the Ceylon Electricity Board (CEB). With the relatively minor exceptions of the State Timber Corporation, which played a limited role in the supply of fuelwood to urban consumers, and of the Department of Census and Statistics, which collected data and presented a few domestic fuel consumption statistics, government institutions scarcely recognized or engaged with the sphere of biomass energy at all.

Early responses
When oil prices increased for the first time, the Ministry of Planning and Employment took initial responsibility for co-ordinating a response. A number of measures to conserve fuel in the industrial and public sectors were taken within a short period, and several committees were established as a first step towards formulating a longer-term response.

The immediate aftermath of the first price increases also

saw a number of isolated attempts by other government and non-government organizations to address problems of domestic energy supply and conversion, most of which revolved around a search for improved technologies. Attempts were made to design stoves, solar water heaters, and biomass generators, but these initiatives attracted little interest beyond the immediate circles in which they were being explored.

The rural energy centre
A more consolidated attempt to identify technical solutions to the domestic and non-domestic energy needs of rural consumers was made with the establishment of a Rural Energy Centre at Pattiyapolla, on the south coast, in 1975. Supported by the United Nations' Development Programme, this conducted further research into stoves, heaters and biomass, and also explored the possibilities of wind power and photovoltaics. Some of the ideas arising from its various research programmes were to achieve a limited measure of popularity, but none were to progress to a mass dissemination phase. Dutch-supported work to promote the use of wind power with the Water Resources Board and elsewhere in the government system achieved a similarly limited impact.[1]

Towards an energy policy
As these efforts were being made, preliminary attempts to formulate a national energy policy were beginning to take shape. Again supported by the UNDP, these may be traced back to 1975, with the creation of a post for Planning in Energy and Environment in the newly established Development Planning Unit of the Ministry of Planning and Employment. Further momentum was provided by the appointment of an Indian adviser in 1977.

A series of papers was duly produced, drawing largely upon existing secondary sources. These dealt mainly with commercial energy,[2] but the primary importance of what was, at that stage, described as wood fuel was now recognized officially for the first time. The possible linkage to wider questions of deforestation was also raised. The findings of the studies were discussed in a national seminar in 1977 and presented in a report which came out in 1978.[3]

Preliminary ideas arising from this work were debated in the 1977 election campaign, when widespread public disquiet at the accelerating rate of deforestation was also articulated for the first time, and these were subsequently to form the basis for policies pursued by the incoming United National Party (UNP) government.

The perceived need for action was then reinforced by the second round of petroleum price increases in 1978, and provided with a clearer sense of direction by the international response which followed particularly the 1981 United Nations Nairobi Conference on New and Renewable Sources of Energy.

The second round of oil price increases: 1978–87

New initiatives
Shortly after coming into power, the new government launched three major energy-related initiatives. The pace of the Mahaweli Hydro-electricity Programme was accelerated.[4] The flow of resources to the forestry sector was rapidly increased, and a forestry resources development project was established. And a series of new energy conservation measures was introduced, as an interim solution, whilst the capacity to increase supply was being developed. The early years of the new government also saw several more small-scale energy initiatives, most of which sought to develop new and renewable substitutes for commercialized industrial and agricultural production.[5]

Both of the major activities which will be reviewed later in the book originate from this period. The CFP (Community Forestry Project), which was planned from 1980 and implemented from 1982 onwards, may be traced back in part to the more general developments taking place in the forestry sector. The stoves programme, on the other hand, has its roots mainly in initial experimental work undertaken by a non-government organization starting in 1979, and was only adopted as an official initiative at a considerably later stage.

Administrative restructuring
As these general and more specific measures began to unfold, moves were also afoot to put new administrative and policy-making structures in place. The first of these was the establishment of the Ministry of Power and Energy (MPE) in 1980. This incorporated the CEB and was placed, for an initial period, under the direct control of the President.

11

Next, in 1982, the former National Science Council was upgraded to the status of a Natural Resources, Energy and Science Authority (NARESA), and initially given responsibility for the formulation of energy policy, although this function was quickly to be transferred to the new ministry. The final major element in the reorganization was completed in 1984, as the MPE assumed control over the Ceylon Petroleum Corporation.

The combined effect of these changes was to create a situation where authority for the formulation of energy policy was drawn together with responsibility for major areas of implementation under the control of a single government institution for the first time.

From 1982 onwards, this position was consolidated through the creation of a number of new posts and structures within the MPE. A Director of Energy Planning was appointed, and an adviser seconded from the World Bank with EEC support. An Energy Co-ordinating Team was formed, and an Energy Planning Unit set up to help it in its work. Three major committees were established, and given responsibility for different aspects of policy.

Energy planning policy analysis
One of these committees dealt exclusively with commercial energy and need not concern us here. The other two included biomass within their brief, and warrant further consideration.

The first of these committees controlled Energy Planning and Policy Analysis (EPPAN), and was allocated five major areas of responsibility. These were to:

o integrate all energy sector activities;
o identify overall objectives of national energy policy;
o define a national energy strategy;
o set up a computerized energy database;
o review disaggregated supply and demand projections for oil, electricity and fuelwood provided by other organizations.

An initial attempt to produce an overall model of the energy economy was completed in 1985, although interim versions were available a year or two earlier, and had already been used to help shape certain courses of action before it was finalized.[6] The model was notable for drawing commercial and biomass fuels together within a common framework for the first time.

The way in which biomass was treated in this exercise was to influence subsequent developments significantly. Four features were of particular importance:

o Only existing data sources were utilized. These included an important study published by Wijesinghe the previous year, which had provided the first accurate, disaggregated and regionally differentiated measurements of different types of biomass fuel consumption;[7] but even so, the general quality of information remained far less adequate than that available for the commercial sector.

o Wijesinghe apart, figures were presented only as national aggregates. No distinctions were made between different types of biomass fuel, and no account was taken either of regional variations in supply and consumption, or of the logistics of matching shortfalls in certain areas with surpluses elsewhere. This served to reinforce the prevalent international perception of energy shortages as a problem confronting all rural people.

o The dynamic aspects of the analysis were derived partly from the untested assumption that consumers, when confronted with biomass energy shortages, would substitute 'upwards' into kerosene.

o The need for action on the biomass front was derived, again at least in part, from the widely held assumption discussed earlier that fuel collection was a major determinant of deforestation.

New and renewable sources of energy
The second committee dealt with New and Renewable Sources of Energy (NRSE), and owed its establishment, and much of its subsequent agenda, to events set in motion by the Nairobi Conference. Its specific brief covered two related areas of activity: to co-ordinate the large number of private and public sector initiatives referred to earlier, which had arisen more or less spontaneously in the wake of the second round of petroleum price increases; and to carry out its own technical, financial and economic reviews of new and renewable possibilities, including financing and other-

13

wise encouraging commercialization where it appeared appropriate to do so.

A biomass strategy?

Although apparently comprehensive in its coverage, this new structure still left significant gaps. The EPPAN model relied upon largely untested data about biomass supply, whilst NRSE concentrated mainly on commercial applications, and had little to say about the much larger domestic sector.

In 1985, a proposal was put forward for a further initiative within the MPE which might potentially have overcome these limitations. Labelled the Biomass Energy Strategy, this was intended to establish a better picture of the interaction between biomass availability and use, and to provide a clearer basis upon which to set priorities across the full range of possible interventions affecting commercial and domestic end uses.[8] But this failed to progress very far, since it was felt that another exercise which had in the meantime been launched by the Forestry Department (FD), to produce a Forestry Master Plan (FMP), would render it largely redundant.[9]

The significance of these observations will be explored further in the concluding section of the chapter.

The major interventions

Whilst the major administrative changes of the post-1978 period were taking place, the two major interventions with which we shall be concerned were already getting under way.

As we saw earlier, the CFP had been started in 1982. Supported by the Asian Development Bank (ADB), and managed within the FD, this proceeded along a largely predetermined path, and was subject to very little influence from the new structures being assembled within the MPE. The full account of its progress is presented in Chapter 5.

With stoves, on the other hand, the position was rather less clear-cut. Government research institutions were involved to a limited extent from an early stage, but the major initial thrust, again as we have already seen, came from a non-government organization. In this case, three years of research and testing led, in 1983, to the identification of a design which was then selected for promotion by the MPE

14

under its National Fuelwood Conservation Programme (NFCP). The MPE did not, however, control sufficient resources to mount a national programme by itself, and was obliged to rely heavily upon the assistance of various donors, which was supplied through the medium of the district Integrated Rural Development Projects (IRDPs) which they were supporting. The course of this programme is described in Chapter 6.

One further initiative must also be mentioned, although this materialized too late to be investigated during field work upon which the research was based. This was the MPE programme to promote stoves specifically for the urban market, which was organized in 1987 in conjunction with the Intermediate Technology Development Group (ITDG) and a group of local manufacturers. This will also be discussed briefly in Chapter 6.

The implications for biomass

Three central conclusions may be drawn from this account, each of which helps to pave the way for an understanding of the course which the forestry and stove interventions were to follow.

Administrative control

Although the early 1980s saw a progressive drawing together of the functions of policy-making and implementation within the newly created MPE, and although biomass was included within its remit, the new institution was never able to exercise the same degree of control in this sector that it enjoyed in relation to commercial energy.

Responsibility for the execution of fuel-related forestry activities lay elsewhere, and was discharged in a largely autonomous fashion. The MPE was, on the other hand, able to exert more influence over the initial stoves programme, which was directed mainly at rural consumers; but key decisions in this instance again rested largely with foreign donors, and with the different part of the government system with which they, in turn, were associated. Only in the case of the later urban stoves programme did it prove possible for the MPE to make policy, and then directly to put it into effect.

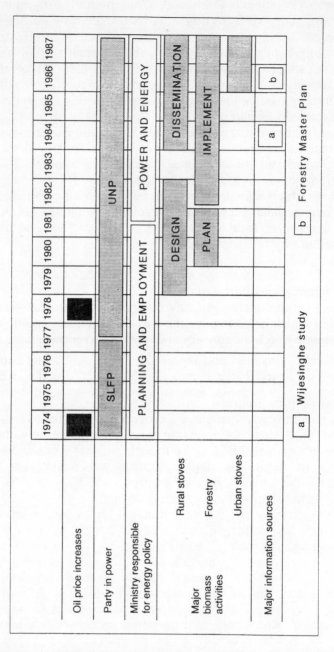

Figure 2.1: *Major biomass-related activities in the context of overall energy policy: 1974–87*

16

The data vacuum

The second major point concerns the generation and utilization of information about biomass. Figure 2.1 indicates that the two major studies, by Wijesinghe in 1984, and the far more comprehensive Forestry Master Plan (FMP) in 1986, were both conducted long after the direction of the Community Forestry Project (CFP) had been determined, and that only Wijesinghe was available when the National Fuelwood Conservation Programme (NFCP) got under way. Only the urban stoves project was able to draw upon both of these sources at the planning stage.

Before these studies were carried out, only rudimentary and rather unsatisfactory information was available. In the case of the CFP, the situation was exacerbated by the fact that it made provision for its own baseline study, but only set this in motion in 1984, and only received the relevant report in 1987. All this meant that key decisions had to be taken largely in ignorance of the nature and extent of the problem which was to be addressed.

Official perceptions

The third feature arises in relation to the way in which biomass is perceived and represented in major documents. In the MPE model it is constructed essentially as if it was another readily isolable, internally homogenous, and hence centrally controllable branch of energy production, with much in common with petroleum and electricity. In the FMP it is treated in a more realistic fashion, but there is still a marked tendency to deal with it in a manner which abstracts from the realities of how it is actually produced and used.

The chapters which follow in the next section will attempt to use the information which is now available to construct a more disaggregated picture of the interaction between biomass demand and supply, and to locate it more firmly within its context.

Notes

1. For a detailed analysis of biogas and wind power, see Greeley (1989).
2. The expression 'commercial energy' will be used throughout the book to refer to petroleum, electricity and other wholly commercially transacted fuels. It is not entirely satisfactory since a small but

growing proportion of biomass fuels are now also commercially transacted.
3. Sankar (1978).
4. This involved the damming of Mahaveli River headwaters in Kandy District to provide power for urban areas and irrigation for largely previously forested areas of the dry zone to the north.
5. National Science Council of Sri Lanka (1982).
6. Munasinghe (1986).
7. Wijesinghe (1984).
8. Ministry of Power and Energy (1985).
9. Ministry of Lands and Land Development (1986).

SECTION II
THE ECONOMIC AND SOCIAL CONTEXTS

3. The national picture

We saw, in Chapter 2, how initial attempts to formulate general energy policy, and to plan specific interventions, lacked all but the most rudimentary data on biomass supply and use. Wijesinghe's 1984 study created a rather better foundation for looking at the demand side of the equation at a more disaggregated level; but it was not until the completion of the FMP in 1986 that figures of a comparable quality became available on biomass production. By combining these two sets of data, and supplementing them with some more minor sources, it is now possible to conduct further analysis, and to arrive at an impression of overall biomass energy balances within individual districts. These balances, in turn, may then be used to assess the extent to which interventions may be required and to determine where they would most appropriately be directed.[1]

The account starts with a brief presentation of essential background information on geography and variations in land use by area. The strengths and weaknesses of the plan and other sets of data are then reviewed. This is followed by descriptions of the major sources of biomass, and of consumption patterns. The chapter then concludes with an attempt to explore the interaction between supply and consumption, to identify areas of likely shortage, and to see which socio-economic groups are most at risk.

The geographical context

Sri Lanka lies between 5° and 10° north of the equator. It is 430 kilometres (km) long and 320 km wide, and has an area of 66000 square kilometres. The island consists of a central hill region, surrounded by more extensive lowland plains. Population is concentrated in the south-western area, which receives rainfall from two monsoons, and is known as the

Wet Zone. Far fewer people live in the Dry Zone, which comprises some two-thirds of the land area, but receives only one monsoon. A narrow Intermediate Zone is sometimes also distinguished.

The country is divided into 25 administrative districts, and it is these which generally provide the basic units within which official statistics are collected and made available.[2] Most districts fall clearly within one or other of the major agro-climatic zones, but a significant minority do not. This has led to some variations in the manner in which the country has been sub-divided in different fuel studies. The system to be followed here is a compromise between the ones used in the FMP and Wijesinghe, and attempts to combine the most useful features of each.

Land use by agro-ecological zone

The low-country Wet Zone

The low-country Wet Zone incorporates three of the five major units into which the country as a whole will be broken down for the purposes of understanding patterns of fuel availability and use.

The first of these is what will be described as the coconut zone. This includes the area immediately surrounding Colombo, where paddy is the dominant form of cultivation, but where substantial areas of land are also devoted to small homestead gardens in which coconuts are grown alongside a range of other less important tree crops. The zone also encompasses the so-called Coconut Triangle further to the north. This comprises the districts of Gampaha, Puttalam and Kurunegala, where mixed home gardens give way progressively to single-cropped plantations as one moves further away from the capital. This unit is completed by the south-western coastal districts of Galle and Matara, which have a more diversified pattern of land use.

The second zone lies to the east and south-east of the capital, on the lower slopes approaching the Hill Country. It is made up of the districts of Kegalla, Ratnapura and Kalutara, where rubber is the major crop. The third comprises the district of Colombo itself, which, by virtue of its high degree of urbanization, stands apart from the rest of this part of the country. Very little forest cover remains anywhere in this region of Sri Lanka.

The Hill Country

The fourth zone is the Hill Country. Tea is the major crop throughout this region, although it is most heavily concentrated in Nuwara Eliya. There is some small-holder cultivation, but the industry is mainly organized in large public sector estates. Falling international demand has led to a reduction in output in recent years and, as a result, extensive areas have been taken out of use and reclassified as sparsely used cropland.

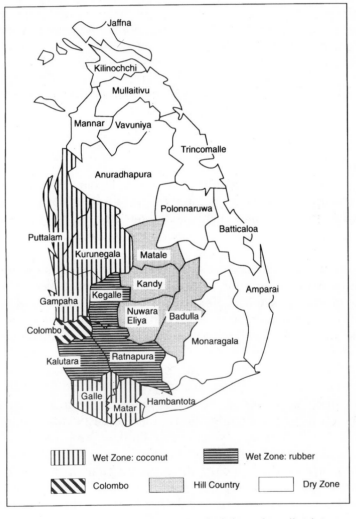

Map 3.1: *Sri Lanka: zones and administrative districts*

In Kandy and Badulla, where tea is a little less important, there are more substantial areas under home garden. At lower elevations, coconuts again tend to figure as the most important individual tree, but substantial quantities of spices, cocoa, coffee and pepper are also found. Higher up, fuel-wood and timber species become more common. Paddy is cultivated in and around river valleys, and other crops, including tobacco and various forms of vegetable, are found in scattered hillside locations.

As in the low-country, forest cover remains, for the most part, sparse, but there are some areas of tropical rain forest in the lower parts of the hills. These give way to tropical highland rain forest above 1000 metres (m), and to mountain forest above 1800m. Cover increases with altitude, and in Nuwara Eliya, the highest district, more than 27 per cent of all land is still under forest. In spite of this, there is little or no potential for further exploitation.

The Dry Zone

'Descending' from the hills to the north, through Matale and Anuradhapura to the east, through Badulla into Monaragala, and to the south into Hambantota, one arrives finally at the Dry Zone, where shifting *chena* cultivation has traditionally been the dominant land-use pattern.

More recently, the Mahaweli project, extending outwards into the Dry Zone from its headwaters in Kandy, has led to the clearance of some 250000 hectares (ha) in Anuradhapura, Polonnaruwa, Amparai and parts of Trincomalee and Badulla.[3] This land has been used for paddy cultivation, complemented by stable upland agriculture. Beyond the Mahaweli, the renovation of ancient irrigation tanks has served to extend the area of paddy cultivation still further.

Largely as a consequence of these developments, the land frontier has been moving northwards and eastwards into the Dry Zone, absorbing an estimated 42000ha each year. Substantial areas still remain under forest in most districts, but at present rates, the belt currently separating the hills from the coastal paddy-growing areas of Amparai, Batticaloa and Trincomalee in the east and Jaffna in the north, will have disappeared almost entirely by 2020.

The overall significance of biomass

Data sources
Forestry products and agricultural by-products are of central importance to Sri Lanka's overall energy supply. Broad estimates suggest that together they account for approximately 67 per cent of gross, and 38 per cent of useful energy consumption. Eighty-eight per cent of biomass fuel is absorbed by the domestic sector, where it satisfies 94 per cent of demand, and the remaining 12 per cent by industry, where it meets 68 per cent of the total requirement.[4]

In order to move beyond these overall impressions to form a more disaggregated picture of the production, distribution and consumption of biomass fuels and in order to lay a foundation for the consideration of likely future trends in availability, it is important to start by asking how reliable the basic data in the FMP and other sources might be.

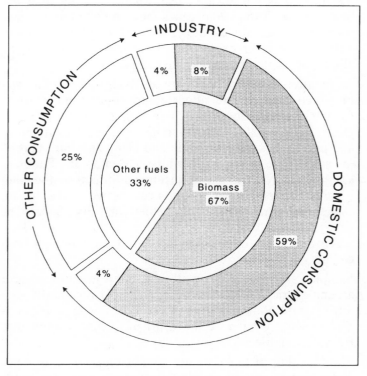

Figure 3.1: *How biomass contributes to Sri Lanka's total primary energy consumption*

Problems of interpretation
The interpretation and comparison of these sources present a number of difficulties:

o Figures for actual present fuel supply in the FMP are only provided at the national level, and there is little explanation of how they were arrived at. They cannot readily be related to the future projections, which are disaggregated to the level of individual sources within districts, and similarly presented on the basis of only partially articulated assumptions. The problem is compounded by the fact that these appear to derive, in some instances at least, from notions of what might ideally happen, as opposed to what might actually be anticipated.

o Researchers vary in the ways in which they classify fuels. Some provide breakdowns by species. But others use general categories, such as crop wastes, and in these instances it is not always clear where dividing lines are being drawn. Tables sometimes include potential overlapping categories, for example, coconut and home garden, without any clear explanation of principles guiding the allocation of items between headings.

o As mentioned earlier, there are also variations in the way in which districts are allocated to zones, and analysts frequently select zones which encompass, and hence disguise, substantial internal variations in fuel availability and use. For example, Matale and Gampaha form part of the same zone in the FMP, whilst Colombo and Puttalam are lumped together in Wijesinghe. Similarly, the plan ignores the significant differences between the urban, estate and rural sectors altogether, and the Survey of Consumer Finances only provides national-level data, leaving Wijesinghe to offer the only breakdown by both category and zone.

o Samples are in general small, and often highly clustered around particular locations. Critical, and potentially distorting omissions therefore arise. Wijesinghe, for example, appears to have excluded urban Colombo altogether from his sample.

o The meaning of tables is not always clear. This is especially a problem in the FMP. For example, in Vol. 5, p.13, under a table entitled 'Distribution of household number

26

by zone and type', a figure of 7 per cent is given for coconut fuel consumption in Colombo, whilst the corresponding figure on the following page, in a table entitled 'Consumption of fuelwood by zone and type', is 41 per cent.

o Due to typographical and mathematical errors, several total and other figures appearing in tables are incorrect. The plan is again the main offender. Readily identifiable mistakes probably represent only a proportion of the total number of errors present.

All this is not to discount the value of the available data. Partially flawed and inconveniently packaged secondary sources are clearly preferable to none at all, and the difficulties of collecting reliable data should not be underestimated. This having been said, the limitations which have been identified necessarily exert a powerful influence both upon what can be attempted by way of further analysis, and upon the degree of certainty with which any conclusions can be arrived at.

Method of analysis
In view of the magnitude of inter-district variations within zones, and of the difficulty in determining how many national and zonal aggregates have been arrived at, the general procedure adopted has been to work from the most disaggregated figures available and to use these as the building blocks from which more general statements may be derived. In practice, this has entailed a heavy reliance upon the FMP for supplying data, and the combined use of the Consumer Finances Survey and the Master Plan Annex V for consumption figures.

The disadvantage in pursuing this particular line of analysis is that there are substantial grounds for believing that these sources are less reliable than Wijesinghe, who unfortunately only presents figures at the zonal level. The impact of this disadvantage has been minimized, wherever possible, by comparing the more disaggregated sources with his findings. Where apparent discrepancies between the two perspectives arise, data have then either been discarded, or presented with qualifications accompanied by speculation as to the directions in which they may err.

27

Biomass fuel production

Overview

The biomass fuel used by domestic and industrial comsumers comes from a wide range of sources. Initially, it is useful to divide these into three broad categories:

○ Those which are exportable, that is of a sufficient physical density, and found in sufficient species concentrations for it to be economically feasible for them to be transported beyond the boundaries of the districts from which they derive. This includes the wood products of the natural forests of the Dry Zone and of the Wet Zone rubber and coconut plantations. This category accounts for by far the greatest portion of fuels which are commercially transacted, and for nearly all industrial biomass fuel consumption.

○ 'Other fuelwood' includes wood which is either smaller (such as the produce of sparsely used cropland), not found in large concentrations (such as home garden and tea shade trees), or some combination of the two. Cinnamon, which is produced on a relatively modest scale, and mainly consumed within the districts where it is produced, has also been placed in this category. These fuels have not been commercialized to any great extent, but provide a product of relatively good quality for domestic use.

○ 'Other fuel' comprises crop wastes, and is made up largely of coconut by-products from plantations and home gardens. In addition, tea wastes are important in the Hills, and palmyrah leaves around Jaffna in the Dry Zone. The low density of crop wastes means that they are nearly always consumed close to the point of production. They are in general less pleasant and convenient to use than other fuelwood.

The supply figures presented in Table 3.1 are based upon estimated total production of materials which may be used as fuel. Where there is an alternative use which always takes precedence over fuel, and from which no fuel remains (for example, logs from a rubber or coconut tree), then the quantities involved have not been included. However, when materials, such as coconut husks or palmyrah leaves,

Table 3.1: Annual potential fuel production by source 1985–90

Category	Fuel source	Production '000 tonnes*	Percentage
Exportable fuelwood[1]	Rubber	2012.1	12.2
	Coconut	204.4	1.2
	Forest	7340.0	44.4
	Sub-total	9556.5	57.8
Other fuelwood	Home garden	898.2	5.4
	Sparsely used cropland	820.1	5.0
	Cinnamon	154.0	0.9
	Tea shade trees	151.0	0.9
	Other[2]	105.0	0.6
	Sub-total	2128.3	12.8
Other fuel	Home garden	1270.4	7.7
	Coconut	2106.6	12.7
	Palmyrah	330.6	2.0
	Tea	920.3	5.6
	Other[3]	131.1	0.8
	Sub-total	4759.1	28.8
	Total	16537.9	100.0

* This, and all subsequent figures, refer to air dry weights.
1. Palmyrah and cinnamon have been excluded from this category since, although in principle exportable, they are only produced in small quantities and consumed locally.
2. This category includes mixed trees and perennial crops, palmyrah, urban land and various other less important sources.
3. This category includes mixed trees and perennial crops, and urban land.

are sometimes used for fuel and sometimes for other purposes, then the total production figure is recorded under fuel supply. This procedure seems sensible, given that the quantities required by these directly competitive end uses are usually relatively small, but difficult to determine with accuracy. The overall effect is for potential fuel supply to be somewhat overstated.

A further point to be borne in mind is that not all exportable fuel can be taken as available to any consumer. In some instances, sources will simply be too inaccessible and/or markets too distant for the fuel to be effectively available. For similar reasons, not all of the fuel included in the non-exportable categories will actually be available to any consumer within the districts in which it is produced. The effect again here is for actual fuel supply to be overstated to some extent.

Potential fuels, such as paddy husks and bagasse from sugar, whose use is presently confined very largely to the post-harvest processing of the products from which they derive, and which account only for a very small proportion of total consumption, have not been taken into account.

The significance of the three major types of fuel varies by zone. A substantial amount of exportable fuelwood is produced by the rubber plantations in the Wet Zone, but coconut wastes predominate, and relatively little other fuelwood is found. The Hill Country produces hardly any exportable wood and only modest quantities of other fuels. In the Dry Zone, the situation is reversed, with large amounts of exportable but only comparatively insignificant amounts of other fuels being produced.

There are also large inter-zonal disparities in the per hectare output of individual fuel. Yields are far higher in the Wet Zone and the Hill Country than they are in the Dry Zone. This goes some way towards negating the effects of imbalances in population densities.

Natural forest sources of fuel
Dry Zone forests consist largely of species such as *weera* and *palu* which are only suitable for fuelwood. This source is supplemented by the unused portions of the less frequently found timber varieties. Extraction is generally organized by private contractors, with the State Timber Corporation performing only a relatively minor role.

The calculation of annual potential forest fuelwood supply for the period 1985–90 involves a number of steps. The starting point is the estimate in the FMP, which appears to be based on the assumptions that fuel will only be available from land which is completely cleared, and that clearances will take place at the rate of 10000ha a year. The estimate, in other words, is a measure of the total stock of fuelwood standing on the areas in question. For the purposes of the present exercise, the hypothetical figure of 10000ha has been replaced by the actual clearance figure of 42000ha and the supply figure adjusted upwards accordingly.

Total supply is then allocated to individual districts in proportion to areas recorded as under forest in 1981. Clearances are presently generating fuelwood at a level which is greatly in excess of demand, and most of what is produced thus goes unused. Present practices cannot be sustained for more than 20 to 30 years, however, and the effect upon fuel supplies is likely to be felt well before the final closure of the land frontier.

Rubber

Rubber trees are generally felled and uprooted at about 30 years of age, and the normal practice is for extensive areas to be clear felled together. About a third of the wood is of saw-log quality and the remainder, in principle at least, is available as fuel. In practice, less than half of the stump, which comprises about 10 per cent of the total volume, appears to be used at present. The work is usually carried out by contractors, who are responsible for all aspects of the operation, from uprooting to distribution. The recent trend of replacing clonal by budded varieties is only likely to lead to a marginal reduction in overall fuel availability in the long run, but the industry has been engaged in a period of unusually rapid replanting, which has maintained supplies at a relatively high level.[5] This is now beginning to decline, however, and is expected to fall to around 45 per cent of its present level by 2010 after which it should start to rise again. The period of decline will coincide with a marked reduction in the quantity of wood available from forests.

Coconut

The average life of coconut trees is approximately 60 years, but clear felling is the exception rather than the rule, making it difficult to arrive at precise figures. Sixty per cent of the trunk is used for timber, with the remainder being left for fuel. The stump adds another 25 per cent to total volume, but is rarely used. Given the length of rotation, the existence of competing end uses and the fact that it does not lend itself well to domestic use, coconut wood is therefore only of minor significance as a fuel. The crop wastes, the husks, leaves and shells, which are produced in significant quantities from about the seventh year onwards, are of far greater significance, and are used extensively in the immediate localities where they are found. Small proportions of each waste have alternative end uses which are more valuable than fuel, and where husks are not required they are utilized as fertilizer. It is clear that a substantial proportion, perhaps

31

20 per cent, of all husks are at present not absorbed by fuel or other more important requirements.

Tea
Fuel is available from uprootings (28 per cent), prunings (58 per cent), and shade trees (14 per cent). Traditional varieties, which will continue to account for virtually all clearances until 2000, have a life of approximately 70 years, and shade trees are removed at the same time, although they may also be pollarded. Nearly all of the wood which they provide is used as fuel, but most trees were removed about 20 years ago in the belief that this would increase yields. This accounts for the relatively small contribution made by this source. Uprootings also appear to be fully utilized. Pruning, which provides more than half of potential supply, generally takes place on a four-year cycle. About half of the produce is not presently utilized as fuel and of this only 20 per cent is recycled as fertilizer.

Home gardens
Home gardens provide fuel from three different sources. The first are the coconut trees. These are most important in the Low Country, but only make a small contribution in the Hill Country districts. As in coconut plantations, the importance of wastes far exceeds that of fuelwood production, but competing end uses account for a smaller proportion of supply. The second source is the fuelwood trees, which progressively displace coconut at higher altitudes, although a small proportion of total production in this category is used for poles. The hedges surrounding gardens are a source of small wood, and contribute to a roughly equivalent extent in all locations. According to the FMP, the area under home gardens is expected to increase by an average of 1.44 per cent per annum as population grows.

Sparsely used cropland
In the Dry Zone, this takes the form of *chenas* (shifting cultivation), recently abandoned *chena* land, or sparsely used rainfed cropland. Elsewhere, it includes neglected or abandoned rubber, tea and coconut areas, and land which is under development. The fuel produced is mainly small bush-type wood, which begins to establish itself some two to three years after cultivation ceases. The stock of land within this

category is constantly being diminished by the extension of home gardens, but, for the time being, is simultaneously replenished by the conversion of forest areas. This can only continue for as long as forests remain, and net reductions are anticipated in the Wet Zone from the early 1990s and in the Dry Zone from about 2010.

Fuel consumption

Domestic
Biomass, as was seen earlier, accounts for 94 per cent of domestic energy consumption. Kerosene and electricity are potential substitutes, but for economic resons these are unlikely to displace it to any significant extent in the foreseeable future. According to Leach, in 1982 the cost per unit of energy delivered from kerosene was five times that of fuelwood,[6] and despite heavy falls in kerosene prices since then, the gap remains large. Electricity is even more expensive, and only 13 per cent of households have mains connections.[7] In 1981, few households with monthly incomes of less than 4000 rupees (Rs) purchased electric or kerosene cookers, and for gas the income threshold was even higher. Only 6.7 per cent of households fall within this bracket,[8] which is far in excess of median monthly household incomes in the range of Rs1000 to 1250.

A geographical concentration of wealth leads to some variation in the relative importance of biomass fuel consumption by district, but it is only in Colombo, and to a lesser extent in Nuwara Eliya, that there are substantial numbers of households which do not depend upon it. The consumption patterns of these two districts are partly a function of difficulties in obtaining fuel, and of the convenience of commercial fuels to urban workers.

Biomass use in the home is confined almost exclusively to cooking and closely related operations, such as boiling water for tea and the preparation of medicinal herbs. Other uses, such as heating water for bathing children or invalids, only arise occasionally in most locations. Others still, such as the parboiling of paddy, ironing clothes, and space heating, are confined to small numbers of households or locations.[9]

Given the relative unimportance of alternative fuel sources, and the broadly homogenous patterns of fuel use, population density is left as the major determinant of the geographical distribution of demand, and only minor variations in per capita consumption arise. Only Colombo, at 1kg a day, falls far below the national average of 1.4kg a day, and only Nuwara Eliya, where consumption rises with low temperatures and the need for space heating, exceeds it to a significant extent. Relatively high levels of consumption are also found in certain Dry Zone districts, where the rate of forest clearance has been particulary rapid, and where there is no need for fuel to be used sparingly.

The types of biomass fuel consumed vary from one part of the country to another. For the most part, there is a close and predictable correlation between local production and use. In the Wet Low Country there is a clear tendency for rubber, coconut wastes and cinnamon use to be concentrated mainly in the areas where they are most extensively cultivated, and the same applies in the case of tea in the up-country estates. By the same token, Dry Zone consumption is dominated by forest wood, with the partial exception of Jaffna, where palmyrah is extensively used. The general pattern only begins to break down in the case of Colombo and Gampaha in the Wet Low Country, and of the non-estate sectors of the Hill Country districts. The reasons for this will become apparent when supply and consumption data are drawn together in an overall fuel balance.

Industrial consumption

Industries only account for 12 per cent of total biomass energy consumption, but are relatively important in relation to the exportable category, from which virtually all of their requirements are met. By virtue of their geographical concentration, they also exert an influence in certain locations which is disproportionate to their overall significance.

Tea consumes far more than any other industry, and is located almost entirely in the Hill Country. Tobacco, which is another fairly heavy consumer, is also mainly concentrated here. Demand is also relatively high in the northern Wet Zone, from bricks and tiles, desiccated coconut and coconut oil, tobacco and rubber. Rather fewer biomass-using industries are found in the southern Wet Zone, and with the exception of bricks and tiles around Anuradhapura, there are few significant industrial users in the Dry Zone.

34

The balance sheet

Distinguishing districts by balance

By combining data on production with those on domestic and industrial consumption, it is possible to arrive at a sense of overall district fuel balances. These can then be used to identify areas where shortages have already arisen, or may be anticipated in the future, if present trends continue.

Table 3.2 illustrates 'overall balances' (that is, total production of fuelwood and currently used types of crop waste, less total consumption from the same categories). It also utilizes the notion of fuelwood balances (that is, total production of fuelwood, less total consumption). Drawing on

Table 3.2: Identifying fuel shortages

Category	District	Zone	Overall balance '000 tonnes[1]	Fuelwood balance '000 tonnes[2]	Price rank
Overall deficit	Colombo	Wet Low	−373	−399	5
	Kandy	Up-country	−333	−436	7
	Gampaha	Wet Low	−228	−210	4
	Nuwara Eliya	Up-country	−176	−292	1
	Badulla	Up-country	−90	−172	2
Fuelwood deficit	Matale	Up-country	4	−34	12
	Matara	Wet Low	71	−85	8
	Galle	Wet Low	77	−52	18
	Jaffna	Dry	81	−172	9
	Hambantota	Dry	111	−9	10
Self-sufficient	Batticaloa	Dry	123	86	5
	Ratnapura	Wet Low	270	56	11
	Kurunegala	Wet Low	774	72	14
Rubberwood exporting	Kalutara	Wet Low	178	177	16
	Kegalle	Wet Low	403	240	13
Fuelwood exporting	Amparai	Dry	591	584	19
	Mullaitivu	Dry	853	808	22
	Polonnaruwa	Dry	808	789	23
	Anuradhapura	Dry	809	792	24
	Monaragala	Dry	1110	1064	17
Potential exporting	Trincomalee	Dry	513	517	20
	Mannar	Dry	570	477	15
	Vavuniya	Dry	578	568	21
	Puttalam	Dry	640	405	3

[1] Includes both fuelwood (eg rubber wood, coconut wood) and crop residues (eg tea clippings, coconut leaves)
[2] Includes only fuelwood

these two sets of figures, and other subsidiary criteria, districts are then divided into the following six categories:

o *overall biomass deficit*: where total consumption exceeds total production, and large amounts of fuelwood must be imported;

o *fuelwood deficit*: where the overall balance is positive, but fuelwood consumption exceeds fuelwood production, suggesting that imports are taking place on a limited scale;

o *self sufficient*: where the overall and fuelwood balances are positive, but where exportable surpluses are small and the district is not a significant source of supply for others;

o *rubber wood exporting*: where the rubber wood surplus is sufficient for the district to export on a significant scale;

o *fuelwood exporting*: where the surplus of other forms of fuelwood is sufficient for the district to export on a significant scale;

o *potential exporting*: where there is a large surplus of exportable fuelwood which is not presently being utilized because more accessible sources are available elsewhere.

Further indicators of relative availability

Taken by themselves, the balances only provide a rather crude and preliminary indication of likely shortages. The accuracy of the data from which they are derived is insufficient for marginal cases to be assigned to particular categories with any confidence, and they reveal nothing about what are often quite significant differences arising within districts. For these reasons, it is also useful to review other indicators.

The first of these is price, in terms of how districts may be ranked by taking an overall average of the annual average district prices for the years 1979–82,[10] and then assigning the first rank to the case where prices are highest, the second to the second highest, and so forth. More recent data are available, but have been disregarded since these have often been seriously distorted by the effects of intensified ethnic confrontation on access to fuelwood. To take an extreme example, Trincomalee, which stands twentieth on the pre–1983 figures, jumps to first in 1984, purely as a result of this factor.

Closely related to price as an indicator of shortage is the

36

proportion of households purchasing fuelwood. This information is provided by Wijesinghe, who presents zonally aggregated, rather than district level data, but in addition provides a breakdown by urban, rural and estate sectors.

Wijesinghe also provides data on the kind of stove used. Two basic models are in widespread use: the highly energy-inefficient simple three-stone type, and the relatively efficient 'open-hearth' type, which has a partially enclosed combustion chamber. If it is assumed that the former will only be used where fuel is in abundant supply, then the frequency with which the latter is encountered seems likely to provide a reasonable proxy of relative shortage.

Identifying shortages

Districts in deficit
Taking all of these factors into account, a fairly clear picture of the current and potential future geographical distribution of fuel shortages emerges.

The first major area of shortage can be identified in the high population density, highly urbanized part of the Wet Low Country, made up of the adjoining districts of Colombo and Gampaha. Although falling within the Coconut Zone delineated by Wijesinghe, consumption here greatly exceeds production, with the deficit being made good by rubber wood from Kalutara and Kegalle, and forest wood from Anuradhapura.

The heavy dependence upon imported fuel is reflected in the relatively high prices which consumers must pay. The proximity of rubber supplies and comparatively low transportation costs exert some modifying influence for the time being, but these districts seem more likely to be affected by future decline in rubber wood availability, and sharper than average future price increases would appear likely. Low-income urban households, with little or no homestead land, will be affected first and most severely.

Moving through Galle and Matara, towards the fringes of the coconut-growing area of the Wet Zone, population densities remain fairly high, and although there is an overall fuel surplus in both instances, both appear to be in slight fuelwood deficit. Broadly the same position obtains in Jaffna, which is the only Dry Zone district where densities are comparable to those of the Wet Zone, and where there is a high degree of urbanization. It seems likely, in this case, that the bulk of fuelwood supplies is obtained from the heavily forested neighbouring district of Mullativu.

With the marginal exception of Hambantota, all of the other districts falling within the overall and fuelwood deficit categories are found in the Hill Country.[11] Further evidence of significant shortages in this zone is provided by the levels of fuel prices, of fuel purchase and of open-hearth cooking-stove use, all of which are higher than in other parts of the country.

A number of factors have combined to bring about this state of affairs. Relatively high population densities lead to substantial demand, and this is then reinforced by the higher than average per capita domestic consumption, associated with the need for space heating at higher altitudes, as well as by the concentration of fuelwood-using industries. Supply, on the other hand, is generally limited by the comparatively low per hectare yields of the major sources. But tea-producing areas provide a marked exception to this general rule, with wastes, which are apparently in abundant supply, cushioning estate workers from the shortages encountered elsewhere.

Deficits here are made good from a number of sources. Kandy is supplied by rubber wood coming up from Kegalle, and forest wood coming down from Anuradhapura and Polonnaruwa. The latter also supply Matale, whilst Polonnaruwa, in combination with Amparai and Monaragala, is also the major source for Badulla and Nuwara Eliya. Declining rubber wood availability will have relatively little effect in the hills, and the intensification of existing shortages will therefore proceed more slowly than in the deficit areas of the Wet Zone Low Country. But prices, which are already high as a result of the long distances and hilly terrain separating sources from consumers, seem likely to rise steadily as the land frontier recedes further to the north and east. Once again, the urban poor will feel the effects most severely, with the proportion affected being greater than elsewhere, given the virtual absence of home garden ownership amongst this group.

In other districts, a lesser degree of shortage may be experienced. Hambantota, which borders the Wet Zone, has experienced a rapid influx of population in recent years and may now have arrived at the point of fuelwood deficit.

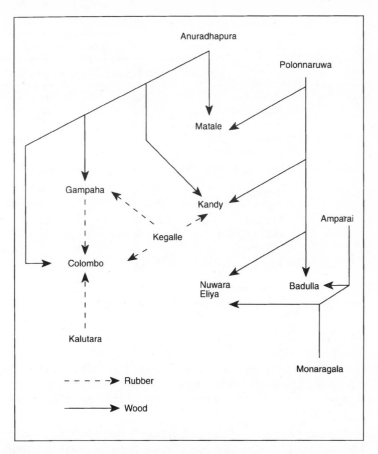

Map 3.2: *Inter-district fuelwood trade*

Puttalam and Batticaloa, whilst clearly not falling within this overall category, have high fuel prices, which would appear to suggest shortages in certain locations at least, although it is not easy to explain why this should be so.

Elsewhere, shortages appear to be confined to the urban sector, especially in the rubber-growing and Dry Zone areas, where home gardens are few in number and/or coconut is not cultivated extensively.

Households at risk

In conclusion, Table 3.3 seeks to identify those likely to be affected, and the numbers involved.[12] Those at highest risk are taken to be the urban biomass fuel purchasers and the

Table 3.3: Groups at risk from fuel shortages

Degree of risk	District	Households (in thousands)	
		Urban buyers	Rural landless
High	Colombo	164	34
	Gampaha	59	82
	Kandy	20	61
	Badulla	6	19
	Nuwara Eliya	4	0
	Sub-total	253	196
Medium	Jaffna	39	31
	Galle	13	41
	Matara	6	41
	Hambantota	6	15
	Matale	5	11
	Sub-total	69	139
Low	Other districts	81	

rural households without land of their own, who live in overall fuel deficit areas. By far the largest concentration within this high-risk category is found in urban Colombo followed, in descending order of importance, by rural Gampaha, rural Kandy, urban Gampaha, urban Kandy and rural Badulla.

Under certain circumstances, it might be considered desirable for those apparently most in need to be further subdivided by income or some other indicator of relative wealth. Such a procedure would seem justified in the light of data presented in the Labour Force and Socio-economic Survey, which show a clear inverse relationship between monthly income and proportion of total expenditure devoted to the purchase of fuel.[13]

Urban purchasers and the rural landless in fuelwood deficit districts are considered to be medium risk. With the exception of urban Jaffna, all of the major concentrations in this case are rural, with Galle and Matara the largest, and Jaffna some way behind. Urban fuel purchasers in zones of overall fuelwood surplus are taken to be low risk.

Remaining households, which together comprise 75 per cent of the national total, are considered to be not at risk. This category is made up of:

- urban households who are wealthy enough to purchase non-biomass fuels, and/or own home gardens from which fuel can be gathered;
- rural households which either own land, or live in zones of surplus where little difficulty is likely to be encountered in gathering fuel from neighbours' or public land;
- all estate households.

In subsequent chapters, it will be possible to compare the actual distribution of fuelwood-related projects with the pattern of apparent needs which have been identified.

Notes

1. This chapter is a modified version of a paper which first appeared in *Biomass* Vol. 19, 1989. The present account will be confined mainly to reporting the major conclusions arising from a lengthy series of calculations. The supporting reasoning and statistics are treated more comprehensively in the paper.
2. There were only 24 when most of the data upon which the analysis is based were collected.
3. See Ministry of Mahaweli Development (1985).
4. Munasinghe (1986). These, and all subsequent figures, refer to primary energy consumption, unless otherwise stated.
5. The supply figures extracted from the FMP fall far below the consumption levels derived from elsewhere. Because the independently arrived-at consumption figure agrees with these consumption levels the original supply figures have been assumed to be incorrect and adjusted upwards to bring demand and consumption into balance through a proportional increase in the supply figures from each producing district.
6. Leach (1984).
7. Munasinghe (1986).
8. Statistics Department (1985a).
9. Wijesinghe (1984) and Ministry of Lands and Land Development (1986).
10. Statistics Department, Central Bank of Ceylon (1985–6).
11. The FMP shows a far smaller deficit for 1985, but anticipated future deficits correspond closely to our present figure. Since the plan does not explain how its own figures are arrived at, the reason for this discrepency cannot be explained.
12. The figures presented are only rough estimates. They have been arrived at by drawing together, and making judgements on data from a variety of sources. They should be treated as no more than approximations to reality, but should still be sufficiently accurate to indicate the relative magnitudes of different categories, and hence the broad priorities which a biomass strategy might pursue.
13. Department of Census and Statistics (1983). Households with a

monthly income of less than Rs300 on average spent 9.3 per cent of their income on fuel. This figure falls steadily through successive economic strata to 3.3 per cent in the case of those with incomes exceeding Rs3000.

4. Fuel production and use in rural communities

Chapter 3 provided a macro-level indication of where bio-mass fuel shortages were likely to arise, and whom they were likely to affect. Chapter 4 explores the interaction between availability and use in six communities where some of the interventions which will be discussed later in the book took place. All are located in the fuel-deficit Hill Country Zone, with three being drawn from Kandy District and the other three from Badulla[1]. This will provide a clearer impression of who is affected by fuel problems, and will also help to explain why certain groups of people suffer when others in the same localities are experiencing little or no difficulty.

The Kandy villages

Location and land use
The first three communites all lie within a radius of 3 km of Mailapitiya in Kandy District, and will be discussed together.

The area falls within the Intermediate Mid-country (IM3) climatic zone,[2] and receives slightly less than 1500mm of rainfall a year. This is concentrated mainly in the *maha* season, which lasts from October to January, but there is also a second minor peak in March or April, which heralds the start of the *yala* season. Hardly any rain falls at all between May and September and little agricultural activity is possible during this period. At this time of year most households find it hard even to obtain the water which they require for domestic purposes. When fieldwork was being carried out during 1986 and 1987, an extended period of drought made life even more difficult than usual.

The village of Mailapitiya lies in a small valley, some

43

12km to the south-east of Kandy, at an altitude of about 700m. Until recently it could be reached by a direct route from the district town, but the road has now been cut by a finger of the reservoir created by the construction of the Victoria dam. The alternative route, which must now be followed, involves a journey of 20 km.

The main part of the village stretches out along the valley floor by the side of the road for a kilometre or so, and peters out a short distance from the water's edge. To either side, valley walls rise quite sharply to heights in excess of 1000m.

The lower slopes, to the east of the road, are covered by mature coconut plantations. At a slightly higher altitude, these begin to thin out, before merging, on one part of the hill, into the small clusters of houses which comprise the hamlet of Alawataketiya. Homes are surrounded by gardens, where a few coconut and other trees grow, and by patches of land which are cleared for seasonal vegetable cultivation.

Further along the hillside, at the same height, lies a larger area of steep, partially terraced land. This is interspersed with sizeable outcrops of rock, and intersected by deep gullies, through which water runs off rapidly during the rainy season. Formerly only used for shifting (*chena*) vegetable cultivation, this has now been converted, under growing population pressure, to annual use. Community forestry plots have been established on a part of this area.

Immediately beyond, one arrives at the neatly laid-out bungalows of the government-sponsored colony of Ihaketiya, each of which is surrounded by a small plot of land. This is the most recently established settlement in the valley, but it lies close to the reservoir. This has led officials to adopt a policy of encouraging, and at times virtually coercing, residents to re-settle elsewhere,[3] so that the hillside can be protected, and the risk of soil erosion and siltation minimized. The picture of the eastern valley slopes is completed by the upper ridges, lying above Ihaketiya and Alawataketiya, which serve mainly as rough grazing land.

The area to the west of the road exhibits a somewhat different pattern of land use. The lower slopes here are devoted almost exclusively to terraced tobacco fields, although a little higher up there is once again an area of home gardens and vegetable patches. This comprises the hamlet of Ketiganawela, and provides the site for the second active community forestry group.

Above that, in turn, is an area stretching to the top of the hill, which has recently been reforested by the forestry project for demonstration purposes. The site of the third forestry group lies a short distance beyond, in the next valley, occupying land which was previously used for vegetable cultivation by farmers from the hamlet of Kurundumulla.

Land tenure

A number of different land tenure arrangements are found in the valley. Most of the area under coconuts is under private control (*sina kara*), and owner operated. Tobacco land is also generally *sina kara* but, in this instance, there are also a considerable number of absentee landlords, who let out much of the area under single crop (*kuli*), or longer-term (*badu*) arrangements.

The status of homestead land on the valley sides is more complicated still. In the longer-established communities, all land was originally cleared and operated under annually renewable government lease (also known as *badu*), but much of this has now been converted to full *sina kara* status. The situation with regard to the remainder is often less than clear, with people feeling that they enjoy full rights, but having no documentary evidence with which to support their claims. In the colony of Ihaketiya, on the other hand, people only have *badu* leases. The remaining upland areas, whether cultivated or not, are all formally Crown Land. Those who choose to work them are held to be encroaching (*anawa sara*) and have no formal legal rights at all.

The low-country Sinhalese élite

The local economy is dominated by a small élite, who are descended from low-country Sinhalese immigrants, and first came to the area in the early 1900s. They live mainly in the central village, but also account for about 10 per cent of all households in the surrounding hamlets (see Table 4.1).

Their strength derives from a number of sources. In the first place, they own most of the coconut land. Second, they also hold some of the tobacco land, and are able to rent rather more; although here, it is not so much land itself, as the ownership of the barns which are used for curing the crop, which provides the key to effective local control of the activity.[4] Renting land, which has recently been cleared

45

Table 4.1: Percentage of households by social class

Community	Kandy			Badulla			Overall
	A'wataketiya	K'ganawela	Kurundumulla	Sapugasdowa	Kanawarella	Nugathalawa	
Rich[1]	15	10		4	13	17	12
Middle[2]	18	41	100	44	44	63	44
Poor[3]	68	49		52	43	19	45
Total[4]	101	100	100	100	100	99	101

1. Rich households share one or more of the following characteristics: owning more land than can be operated by household labour and relying mainly on hired labour, or renting out to others; running a business with hired labour; engaging in some form of professional employment.

2. Middle households share one or more of the following characteristics: owning and operating their own land (labour may be (a) hired in, (b) hired out or (c) performed on rented land, but where this occurs, neither option exceeds work done by household members on their own land); engaging in some form of craft occupation on a self-employed basis; engaging in some regular, semi-skilled form of employment.

3. Poor households share one or more of the following characteristics: work performed on rented in land exceeds work on own land; engaging in casual labour on farms, estates or elsewhere, to a greater extent than work performed on own land.

4. Totals may not always add up to 100 per cent due to rounding.

46

under the Mahaweli scheme in Dry Zone areas to the north of Kandy, for paddy, chilli or vegetable cultivation in the *yala* season, provides a third important source of income for this group.

Finally, over and above their agricultural activities, these relatively rich households may also generate income from a range of contracting, transporting and retailing activities. In addition, they are prominent in local institutions, and are able to draw on contacts with a range of external agencies to secure favourable access to credit and other inputs. They may also engage in various forms of professional employment.

In combination, this enables members of the group to enjoy a much higher standard of living than most of the other inhabitants of the valley. This is reflected in the standard of their houses, which are constructed of brick and concrete, with tiled roofs. All have electricity, and a combination of wells and stand-pipes provide a fairly reliable supply of water.

The labourers
At the other end of the spectrum are the poor households. They comprise between two-thirds of the population of Alawataketiya, where they are most heavily concentrated, and at least half of all of the other communities surrounding the main village. Some of these people are Tamils, whose ancestors came to the valley as labourers on the coffee and cocoa plantations, which formerly occupied the land now allocated to coconuts. Others are more recent lowland Sinhalese immigrants. Others still are the descendants of earlier settlers now obliged, by lack of space on the valley floor, to move upwards to find land upon which to build their houses.

Most own no land beyond their small home-garden plots and, given only limited opportunities to supplement this through encroaching or renting, casual labour for the larger coconut and tobacco growers has to provide the major source of their income. Wages for men who are generally engaged only for cultivation activities, are Rs25–30 a day. Women, who perform both agricultural work and post-harvest sorting of tobacco, command between Rs15 and 20. These employment opportunities are heavily concentrated in the main cultivation season. In addition, a few people are able to obtain off-season work pounding tobacco. Some also travel

47

Table 4.2: Average area of land owned and operated per household by social class (hectares)

Community	Kandy			Sapugasdowa	Badulla		Overall
	A'wataketiya	K'ganawela	Kurundumulla		Kanawarella	Nugathalawa	
HOME GARDEN[1]							
Rich	0.90	0.25		0.15	0.16	0.35	0.44
Middle	0.56	0.31	0.26	0.23	0.22	0.22	0.27
Poor	0.20	0.23		0.33	0.12	0.08	0.21
Overall	0.36	0.26	0.26	0.28	0.17	0.22	0.26
OWN PADDY							
Rich	0.07			0.46	1.04	0.73	0.50
Middle			0.02	0.18	0.13	0.10	0.09
Poor				0.02	0.05	0.02	0.02
Overall	0.01		0.02	0.11	0.21	0.19	0.10
RENTED PADDY							
Rich				0.04	0.07	0.07	0.04
Middle		0.01	0.03		0.02	0.06	0.03
Poor					0.06	0.06	0.02
Overall		0.01	0.03	0.02	0.04	0.06	0.03
HIGHLAND OWNED							
Rich	0.68	2.12		0.05	0.43	0.28	0.65
Middle	0.04	0.16			0.01	0.12	0.07
Poor	0.04	0.02			0.02		0.02
Overall	0.13	0.30	0.03	0.02	0.07	0.12	0.12
H'LAND OTHER[2]							
Rich	0.18	0.30		0.10		0.02	0.10
Middle		0.09		0.11		0.05	0.05
Poor	0.07	0.06	0.01		0.04	0.02	0.04
Overall	0.08	0.10	0.01	0.05	0.01	0.04	0.05

1. In almost all instances, this land is owned.
2. This category is mainly made up of land held under short-term lease. In Kanawarella and Sapugasdowa it also includes very small areas which have been encroached upon.

48

daily to work in the paddy fields in neighbouring districts, whilst others may migrate temporarily to the Mahaweli areas. The majority, however, must rely heavily upon government food stamps to guarantee their survival during the agricultural off-season.

The middle class

Between the small élite, and the near landless majority, is a middle stratum of Sinhalese and Tamil households, who depend, either individually or in combination, upon small tobacco barns, smallholdings of tobacco and vegetable land, and regular employment and self-employment in off-farm activities. Overall, they comprise about 25 per cent of the population, although the proportion varies considerably from one hamlet to another.[5]

Social and political relations

Superimposed upon these economic differences is a further series of social groupings, of which the division between Sinhalese and Tamils is the most significant. In the past, these ethnic groups have enjoyed harmonious relations. Even now, there is still evidently no discrimination in access to local employment opportunities, and many other examples of inter-ethnic co-operation could be cited. Despite all of this, however, it has proved impossible for local relations to be insulated entirely from the broader currents of national politics.

These have fuelled a growing sense of insecurity in the Tamil community, and several households have left the area as a result. Others, whilst remaining, no longer feel able to seek land for rent or to venture far beyond the immediate localities in which they live. Those who have stayed suffer from various forms of discrimination, being excluded from electoral registers, and receiving low priority in the allocation of officially controlled resources.

Kinship provides another building block for social relations, although the various historical influences to which the valley has been subjected have left it with a complicated and somewhat unusual composition, where kinship ties figure less strongly than elsewhere. Networks of relations exist, but are comparatively small, especially in the most recently established colonies. As a result, the area lacks the strong communal cohesion which is typical of the region as a whole.

This is reflected in the fact that virtually all production activities, above the level of the individual households, are conducted on a cash basis. Hardly anyone engages in reciprocal, or in other unpaid forms of work. Various forms of voluntary self-help organizations, such as the death societies, have been established to compensate for the weakness of traditional institutions, but the lack of firm, traditionally based authority is said to have led to atypically high levels of lawlessness, and anti-social behaviour.

Access to fuel

The significance of some of the social and other factors which have been discussed will not become fully apparent until key interventions are explored in the chapters which follow. However, much of the material presented has direct and immediate implications for fuel availability and use.

When the valley was first settled, fuelwood was readily available from the middle slopes, but this source was eroded by expanding settlement, and then virtually eliminated by the heavy demands imposed by the tobacco industry. The Ceylon Tobacco Company, which has a depot in the village, now arranges for fuelwood to be transported into the village for this purpose, whilst domestic users have turned to a range of other sources.

Of these, the by-products of coconut trees growing in home gardens are by far the most important (see Table 4.3 and supporting graphs). In Alawataketiya, where home gardens are largest, the great majority of even the poorest households are able to satisfy most of their requirements from this source. In the neighbouring community of Ketiganawela, by contrast, the average size of gardens is appreciably smaller, and whilst most of the better-off households remain self-sufficient, the majority of the poorest group here must rely mainly upon other people's gardens. The third location in this group is the only one in which common land features significantly as a supplementary source, although in interpreting this result it should be borne in mind that a far smaller, and less representative group of households was interviewed in this case.

Table 4.3: Percentage of households obtaining fuel from different sources by social class[1]

Community	Kandy				Badulla		Overall
	A'wataketiya	K'ganawela	Kurundumulla	Sapugasdowa	Kanawarella	Nugathalawa	
PURCHASED							
Rich	0	0		0	14	56	19
Middle	9	0	8	5	8	33	14
Poor	0	0		70	0	0	6
Overall	2	0	8	2	6	44	11
OWN GARDEN							
Rich	89	75		50	57	44	65
Middle	91	56	50	24	21	45	43
Poor	79	47		48	17	10	50
Overall	82	54	50	38	24	38	48
OTHER GARDEN							
Rich	11	25		0	0	0	6
Middle	0	44	17	0	0	9	10
Poor	12	58		0	0	10	14
Overall	10	49	17	0	0	8	12
TEA ESTATE							
Rich	0	0		50	14	0	6
Middle	0	0	0	62	71	0	26
Poor	0	0		24	83	0	21
Overall	0	0	0	42	69	0	21
OTHER[2]							
Rich	0	0		0	0	0	0
Middle	0	0	25	10	0	12	8
Poor	10	0		28	0	10	10
Overall	6	0	25	19	0	10	8

1. Only information relating to the most important individual source used by each household has been used in this analysis. Subsidiary sources have been ignored.
2. This includes fuel from uncultivated Crown Land, cultivated highland and sawmill by-products.

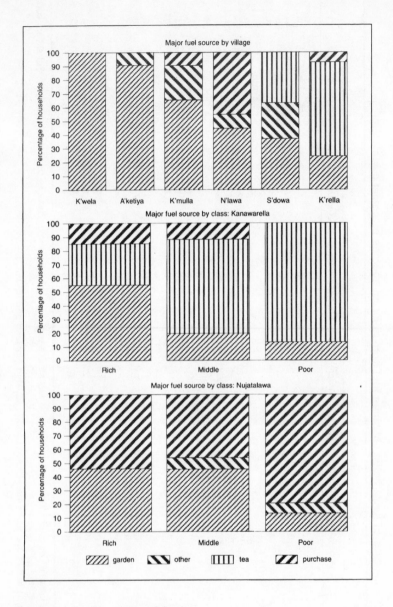

Figure 4.1: *Sources of fuel*

Collection time

How significantly do these differences in access affect people's lives and economic well-being? To answer this question, we must take a closer look at how fuel is obtained from different sources, and see who is responsible for this work. It will also be necessary to ask how much time is involved, how this is distributed through the year, and how far fuel-related activities may impinge upon other things which people do.

Although coconut is the major source of fuel in the Kandy communities, the picture is complicated by the fact that the tree supplies several types of fuel, each of which is gathered and processed in different ways.

Some activities are concentrated around May and June, when most harvesting takes place. As the nuts are plucked, the dead branches, petiole, spathe and flowers are removed and cut into small pieces ready for storage. Husks are removed and cut at the same time. The tree also provides dead leaves and other residues which may be collected throughout the year. Some households spend small amounts of time gathering and cutting these fuels every day. Others, especially those who rely upon other people's home gardens, perform these tasks less frequently. Some process the materials daily, but collect less regularly.

With the exception of de-husking, which is done by male family members, or hired labour in the case of larger holdings, women do most of the work, although men and children will also sometimes help. The amount of time which households require for collection and processing varies according to the balance between the methods used and a range of other factors. It is difficult to measure precisely but, on average, it is unlikely to exceed half an hour a day. The peak input occurs at a time when little else is going on, and the ease with which coconut products can be stored provides a high degree of flexibility in the timing of collection and processing during other periods of the year.

Whereas coconut products come mainly from home gardens, other, less frequently used fuels, may be collected from a range of sources. The fallen branches of *jak* and other home garden trees are gathered in much the same way as coconut wastes, although processing takes rather longer. From time to time a tree will also be cut down, and all of the parts which are not suitable for timber then used. Trees

53

and hedges growing in the vicinity of tobacco and vegetable plots, which are pollarded from time to time to eliminate shade, provide a further source. So do albecia poles which have reached the point where they can no longer be used as frames for vegetable cultivation.

This concludes the discussion of the situation in the Kandy villages. Each of the three Badulla villages will now be considered with the same broad issues in mind.

Sapugasdowa

Location and land use

The first of these is Sapugasdowa, which falls within the Intermediate Up-country (IU3) zone, and has an annual average rainfall of just over 1900mm. This makes it considerably wetter than Maliapitiya, but distribution is similar, with a heavy concentration in the *maha* season from October to January, a smaller peak in April, and other months remaining relatively dry.

The village lies a short distance to the north-west of Badulla town, and can be approached by a network of small, mainly unsurfaced, roads which wind their way for 10km through the upper reaches of a series of adjoining tea estates. Alternatively, by taking a slightly longer route, it is possible to complete almost the entire journey by tarmac road.

Following this route, the traveller arrives first at the small township of Kandegedera, and then takes a mud track which runs down through a string of small communities, before rejoining the main road a little further to the east.

A short distance beyond the path there is a small river, which is flanked by a narrow strip of relatively fertile and privately owned paddy land. This is watered by perennial streams which run down the hillsides. As a result, almost the entire area can be double cropped, although *maha* yields tend to be rather better than those which can be achieved in *yala*, and many people prefer to cultivate a vegetable crop in the second season.

Immediately above the paddy, on the first part of the lower slopes, lies a more extensive area of home gardens. These are also privately owned, and are mainly set aside for the cultivation of timber and fruit trees, including *tuna*, *sapu*, *jak*, avocado, mango and arica. Partly as result of assistance

54

provided by the Department of Minor Export Crops, many households have also been encouraged to grow a little coffee and pepper. In addition, some people have set aside small areas for rainfed vegetables, of which cabbage appears to be the most popular. The gardens are generally small, rarely exceeding 0.25ha.

Most of the houses here are permanent, but a considerable number of semi-permanent structures are also found. None has electricity, and although access to water is not a very serious problem, some families have to walk up to half a mile to obtain their supplies, because an earlier system, which supplied piped water to all houses, has fallen into disrepair.

Further up the hillside is an area of poorer sandy and highly eroded soils, which is mainly Crown Land. Formerly set aside only for chena, some of this has now passed into the hands of private smallholders, who use it for tea and tobacco cultivation. A larger portion has been converted into over-flow homestead land, with 99-year leases being granted to the occupants.

Most of the houses here are only semi-permanent, reflecting the generally lower incomes of their inhabitants. The gardens are scattered about the hillside, and are much poorer than those lower down. There are a few trees, but owing to the relative infertility of the soils, self-propagation does not occur, and trees will only grow where fertilizer has been provided. Otherwise, this land is mainly set aside for producing small crops of pulses and cowpeas.

There is also a substantial area of Crown Land which has remained under patana grassland. Prior to the establishment of the CFP, some previously cultivated land had also reverted to this form. The area has traditionally been used for grazing, being burnt off annually in the dry season to produce fresh grass for the cattle, which form an important component of the local economy. The picture is completed by the tea estates, which cover most of the upper, and more gently sloping part of the hillside.

Economic and social relations
With the exception of the township, where there are some Muslims and low-country Sinhalese, the population of the area is almost exclusively up-country Sinhalese. Amongst this group, the cultivator caste is predominant, but there are

also minorities from a number of lower castes, who live separately in their own small hamlets.

The general standard of living is a little higher than in the communities surrounding Mailapitiya, but a relative shortage of land makes the area the poorest of the three studied in Badulla.

Only a third of all households own any paddy land, and few holdings exceed half a hectare in size. Plots are mainly cultivated by family labour, and few households are wealthy enough to hire more than a small proportion of the total labour required. With the exception of small plots, which have become so subdivided that their owners no longer consider it worthwhile to cultivate them, hardly any land is available for sharecropping. Home gardens are either also very small, or situated on relatively unproductive land, and only a few households enjoy access to any other highland for cultivation purposes (see Table 4.2).

Only 4 per cent of all households could be classified as rich, and although they practise paddy, home garden and, more occasionally, other forms of highland cultivation, these are nearly always combined with professional employment or business activities. Of the latter, retailing is the most common, but a few tobacco barns also continue to operate, although on a far more limited scale than hitherto. Members of this group are the only people in the area who hire labour on a regular basis.

At the next level in the economic hierarchy, there are some households which survive solely from their own agricultural resources, eking out an existence from their paddy fields, home gardens and animal husbandry. Others do not engage in agriculture at all beyond a little home garden cultivation, but rely instead upon work outside the village as drivers, carpenters and in other relatively secure forms of employment. Taken together, these groups broadly define the middle economic stratum in the area, and account for slightly less than half the total population.

The remaining households, which comprise just over half of the total population, have little or no paddy land, and rely primarily on labouring for their livelihoods. Since relatively few employment opportunities arise within the village itself, this usually entails work on the tea estates, where men receive a wage of Rs25 a day, and where women are paid Rs22.

The lack of opportunites has led many people to leave the village altogether. A number of young men have joined the army. Others migrate seasonally for agricultural work in the newly developed Dry Zone areas of Mahiyangana and Giranderakotte.

These circumstances leave little scope for the formation of strong internal economic bonds, either through labour-sharing between equals, or by means of wage labour and tenancy. With the exception of caste-based death societies, there is little by way of social mutual-support institutions either. Finally, the high degree of dependence upon external economic opportunities is reflected in a relatively low level of internal political organization. There are no leaders who are capable of exerting significant influence beyond the village.

The availability and use of biomass fuel

Patterns of fuel availability and use are rather different from those found in Mailapitiya. Home gardens are smaller, and fuelwood productivity declines as coconut gives way to other types of tree. This source can therefore not be relied upon to the same extent, even in the case of the comparatively well off.

A significant proportion of households of all categories uses clippings from the tea estates to make good the deficit, but this is especially true of those in the middle of the economic hierarchy. The poor, whose homes cluster to a disproportionate extent on the higher slopes, tend to have rather larger gardens, as well as being able to satisfy a part of their requirements from Crown Land close by.

The greater diversity of sources is reflected in a more complicated set of arrangements for fetching and processing fuel. Where home gardens are used, it may be gathered in one of two ways. In some cases, women collect the fallen branches of *tuna*, *sapu*, *jak* and mango trees. One informant reported that she spent an average of an hour a day on this activity, with an additional 15 minutes being required for processing.

In other instances, where gardens have *Gliricidia* or *mara* hedges, or guava trees, these are pruned annually, and provide a more convenient source of fuel. One household, which satisfied nearly all of its requirements in this way, reported that the basic work of pruning, further cutting and storage could be accomplished in six person days each year,

57

part of which was hired, and part domestic and that an additional hour per week of household women's time was then needed for final processing.

Opportunities to obtain fuel from the neighbouring tea estate, the most important individual source for the village, arose only in August, when bushes were pruned and in October, when the pruning of shade trees took place. Women and men would go together to collect these fuels, making two or three two-hour trips a day during the short periods when they were available, and building up supplies which might last for up to half of the year. For those already working on the estate, who would be making the trip anyway, the additional time involved was quite small.

On the *patana* grasslands, sticks are gathered from shrubs and guava trees. In some cases, reproducing the pattern found in home gardens, the twigs and branches are collected throughout the year. This is relatively convenient for those living close by, as in the case of one woman who could gather her household's requirements in two half-hour trips a week, and then finish all further processing in an additional hour. Others reported that rather longer round trips were required, although these were probably exceptional. In other cases, fuel was collected from the *patanas* after the grass had been burnt off in the dry season in May. Once again, this was usually women's work. In three days it was said to be possible to gather and transport supplies for two months, with an extra day being required for processing.

Kanawarella

Environment and land use
Kanawarella is the second of the three locations investigated in Badulla district. Average annual rainfall here is about 2300mm, making it rather wetter than Sapugasdowa, although again with a similar distribution. The terrain is very steep, which creates a constant danger of landslips during the wetter months. Five village houses have been destroyed in this way in recent years.

The community lies in a deep valley, close to the border with Monaragala, approximately 20km to the south-east of Badulla. It is approached by a small road which leaves the main road from Badulla to Ella at an altitude of 1100m, runs down the short distance through the tea-covered hillside to the paddy fields on the floor of the valley 150 m below, and then climbs away again on the far side, to rejoin the main road a kilometre or two later.

The valley floor is unusually wide, and provides ideal conditions for paddy cultivation. This places the community at an unusual advantage in an area where such land is at a premium. It has also proved possible to terrace and cultivate parts of the lower slopes as well as areas around streams higher up the valley side. Most land is double cropped.

The *maha* crop entails a relatively low degree of risk, and offers moderate yields. Cultivation begins on the upper slopes in October and November, but is delayed by a month on the valley floor, so as to stagger demand for water. Harvesting then takes place from February to early March. The minor *yala* season follows a similar pattern, with transplanting in February and March, and harvesting in June and July. Yields here can sometimes be higher than in *maha*, but lower rainfall means that cultivators face a higher risk of crop failure.

Home gardens occupy the lower slopes immediately above the paddy fields. They are generally surrounded by thick shrub fences, and contain a diversity of species, including aricanut, *kitul* palms, *jak*, bananas, *sapu* and *tuna*. The trees form a dense canopy through which little sunlight can penetrate, and with the exception of a few patches of beans, little vegetable cultivation is practised. The average plot size is only 0.17ha, which is smaller than that of any of the other communities studied. Between the home gardens is a small number of larger plots, which are mono-cropped with tea, *jak* trees or eucalyptus.

All of the land up to this level is privately owned, but higher up the trees start to give way to more open Crown Land. One section, immediately above the gardens, was allocated under Land Development Ordinance by the last Sri Lanka Freedom Party (SLFP) government to one of its supporters, and is planted with *mara* grass, which provides material for roofing. A rather larger area is cultivated as state-owned land on lease, and is used mainly for vegetables, maize and *kurakkan*. A small amount of land has also been encroached for similar purposes. Sugar was once grown here, but as prices have declined this has virtually disappeared.

Part of the community forestry site now occupies this land.

The remainder extends into the highest slopes, which otherwise are mainly patana grasslands, and serve as communal
grazing land for the sizeable cattle population, which is
retained to plough the paddy fields.

Economic and social relations

Kanawarella is a traditional village with an exclusively
Sinhalese population. Most people belong to the cultivator
caste, and are at least loosely related to each other. There are
also a few households from the lower status drummer and
blacksmith service castes.

The large area of paddy land helps to support living
standards, which are noticeably higher than in any of the
other communities considered thus far. Visible signs of this
are easy to detect. About two-thirds of all houses fall within
the permanent category, with tiled roofs, concrete walls and
floors, and more than half enjoy access to electricity. Water
is readily available from spouts fed by a pipeline running
from a nearby hilltop, which villagers laid nearly 40 years
ago. The community benefits from the surfaced road which
was completed in the early 1980s, and is connected by a
daily bus service to nearby towns. It has a rice mill, a
weaving workshop and a saw mill. Three shops, and three
primary schools also lie within its boundaries.

Within this context of overall prosperity, there are considerable variations in individual wealth, which stem primarily from differences in access to paddy land. The village is
dominated by one man who is said to own 10ha of paddy,[6]
most of which is given out under seasonal or annual sharecrop arrangements.

The same person has a further 6ha of highland. This is
mainly planted with eucalyptus, and is maintained by small
numbers of hired labourers. He also owns saw and rice mills,
which employ some 25 people, and is heavily involved in
contracting work beyond the village. He is a Justice of the
Peace and is Gramodaya Mandala chairman, with a network
of powerful political connections extending well beyond the
immediate locality.

No one else can compete with this dominant individual,
but there are a number of other households with paddy
holdings, which exceed subsistance requirements, and other
highland holdings apart from their homestead gardens. Members of this group hire a major portion of the labour required

60

to cultivate their land, and often engage in professional employment beyond the village.

Next in the hierarchy comes a mainly self-sufficient middle stratum, which comprises slightly less than half of all households. Members of this group have small paddy holdings, which may be supplemented, in some instances, by land taken under temporary sharecrop arrangements. They only rarely hire labour, and rely instead upon a combination of self-cultivation and labour-sharing (*attam*). They may also enter the labour market from time to time to augment their income from land.

The picture is completed by another group, of approximately the same size, which owns no more than a little home garden land.[7] Members support themselves mainly by labouring in the neighbouring tea estates, supplemented by more occasional employment within the community itself, and the share cropping of paddy land.

Male labourers receive Rs25–30 a day, and women a little less. Work on the estates is said to be becoming more difficult to find as chemicals displace the labour that was previously required for weeding. At the same time, employment opportunities within the village are becoming scarcer since there is little additional land which can be brought under cultivation to satisfy the needs of an expanding population. However, with the exception of several of the poorest households, which have sent sons to join the army, there is, at present, relatively little migration.

It will be evident from other aspects of the account that this is, in many respects, a more cohesive community than those considered earlier, with a greater capacity for collective action of different kinds.

Access to fuel

As far as fuel use is concerned, Kanawarella is similar to Sapugasdowa, although the rich households are rather more likely to be self-sufficient, whilst other classes tend to rely more heavily upon the tea estates.

Home gardens provide a combination of regularly available fuel, in the form of fallen twigs and branches, and more periodic supplies from pruning and occasional felling. Clippings are collected from the tea estate in much the same way as in Sapugasdowa, although the competing demand for labour from *maha* paddy cultivation is greater.

But for the minority of households, which are unable to satisfy most of their requirements from their gardens or tea clippings, conditions here are also more difficult. Those falling into this category are left with two alternatives: either they can collect the fallen branches of the trees growing in the forest land which has been set aside by the Janata Estates Development Board (JEDB) or they can gather fuel from the small bushes growing on the *patana* lands and stream sides around the village. Both these sources are scattered, and thus time-consuming to use. It is reported that one person must spend between two and four mornings a week in order secure sufficient supplies in these instances.

Nugathalawa

Environment and land use

Nugathalawa, like Kanawarella, stands at an altitude of about 1000m, although the topography here is undulating, with the land rising gently away to either side to a height of 1200m. It also falls within the same broad climatic zone, with a similar seasonal rainfall distribution, but receives only an average of 1500mm, which is some two-thirds of the Kanawarella total. A particular feature of the climate is the very high winds which are experienced in the dry period from May-July. This means that, in addition to their other functions, trees are also planted as wind-breaks.

The community is located 40km to the west of Badulla, some 5km beyond the small Assistant Government Officer (AGO) town of Welimada, on the way to Nuwara Eliya. The larger part of the village is set among mature home gardens to the south side of the road. Facing it, to the north, lies the middle-class housing estate of Divurumgama, which has recently been developed, under the Village Re-awakening Scheme, on land previously belonging to a private tea company. Two dirt tracks run back from the main road to either side of Divurumgama, the first leading to the smaller community of Girambe, and the second to the recently established colony of Siripura, some two-thirds of a mile back from the road.

A small river flows immediately to the south of the main settlement, providing irrigation for a narrow band of land in the *maha* season. This is joined by a tributary, at the western extreme of the village, which serves a more extensive area of paddy running away from the road to the north. These areas are cultivated under permanent tenure, and are mainly double cropped. Until quite recently, the normal rotation would see *maha* paddy followed by local vegetables in *yala*, but the latter have now been displaced by potatoes, which are produced mainly for the Colombo market.

Traditional vegetable cultivation continues on home garden plots, and in areas of privately owned upland immediately adjoining the community. Beyond this area lies an expanse of land which belonged to a tea estate until the early 1970s, and was then returned to Crown Land status under a Land Reform Act.

Since that time, it has been farmed by different groups of encroachers. Initially, some SLFP supporters were granted informal access when their party was in power, but they were then subsequently displaced by followers of the present government, following their success in the 1977 election. This has proved to be a valuable gain, since most of the area can now be used to double, and sometimes even triple, crop potatoes and other exotic vegetables, which offer very high cash returns.

In addition to the area now devoted to potatoes, a smaller part of the old tea estate had, until recently, remained under tree cover, but this has now been cleared and allocated under the CFP.

Economic and social relations

The social composition of the area is mixed. Up-country Sinhalese make up the largest individual group, but there are also significant minorities of low-country Sinhalese, Tamils and Muslims.

Nugathalawa is, by a considerable margin, the wealthiest of the communities studied. Although crowded closely together, most houses are built to a good standard, and a high proportion fall within the permanent category. Everybody close to the road has access to piped water and electricity, and whilst power lines and water pipes do not stretch far into the interior, even here, all homes have a well within easy walking distance. The main village has a primary school, and there is a secondary school at Keppetipola Township, a kilometre or so down the road.

This prosperity is only partially a function of favourable

conditions for vegetable cultivation. Whilst agriculture contributes, to some extent, to the incomes of the great majority of households,[8] it is the primary source in only about a third of all cases. In seeking to understand how the economy functions, and to explain how the population is differentiated, it is therefore necessary to focus initially on the contribution of non-agricultural livelihoods.

These fall into a number of categories. Many households rely on self-employment, running small brickfields, or working as masons or in other craft occupations. Others work for the State Timber Corporation, which has a large saw mill and timber yard in neighbouring Keppetipola, or in the enterprise making railway sleepers which the corporation supplies. Opportunities for employment, in a professional or semi-professional capacity, are unusually good as a result of the close proximity of the administrative centre of Welimada.

Taking both agricultural and non-agricultural sources of income into account, a number of economic strata may be identified. The most powerful positions are enjoyed by a small group of predominantly Muslim families, who own lorries. Their wealth derives primarily from serving the Colombo vegetable market with potatoes, with the haulage of timber and other building materials providing a subsidiary source of income.

Beneath this group, but still in the 'rich' category are households that depend exclusively upon agriculture. Generally owning both paddy and highland, they often supplement their holdings by sharecropping further land. They rely heavily upon hired labour, and enjoy incomes amounting to several times their subsistence requirements.

Next comes a middle stratum, which employs a variety of resources and economic strategies. At their simplest, these can entail a household neither owning nor cultivating any agricultural land, but surviving simply on some stable form of employment or trade. The category also includes those with landholdings falling within the subsistence range which, given high soil fertility and multiple cropping possibilities, might be as little as 0.25ha. Some households combine these two different types of activity.

At the bottom of the spectrum are those with few agricultural or other resources to their name, beyond the small plots of land on which they live. Most members of this group, which comprises about a fifth of all households, must rely upon agricultural, or other forms of temporary labour for their survival, although this may be combined, in some cases, with the taking of small pieces of land in share-cropping or under cash-rent tenancies.

Taken as a whole, the nature of the local economy, with its high degree of monetization and urban influence, now offers comparatively good opportunities for most households. At the same time, however, the process of economic development which has taken place has encouraged a more individualistic lifestyle, and served to weaken communal bonds. A number of new single-purpose institutions has arisen in their place, but these have not proved particularly successful. As a result the community lacks both strong internal political allegiances and effective leadership.

The availability and use of biomass fuel

Twenty years ago, it is likely that the people of Nugathalawa would have obtained their fuel in much the same way as the present-day inhabitant of Kanawarella, but the conversion of the estate area to housing and other uses has eliminated tea clippings, and the forest which covered parts of the estate land, as potential sources. As a result, households at all points in the economic hierarchy now mainly purchase their fuel, with the tendency being particularly pronounced amongst the poorest.

With the exception of a small minority of rich households, which can afford electricity, people obtain fuel in the form of wastes from the cutting of *tuna* and other trees from the State Timber Corporation depot at the neighbouring township of Kappatiyawa. Wood is sold in 5kg bags which cost Rs2.75 each. A typical household reported that it purchased five bags a week, and then had to pay a lorry driver a further Rs5 or 10 to transport them home, when no one could be found to do it for free. A morning was usually devoted to this task, although other things could also be done at the same time.

In view of the relatively high cost of fuelwood, however, several households prefer to utilize the sawdust which is also produced as a by-product at the depot. Until only two months before our investigation, this had been given free of charge. Now it is sold in 15kg bags which cost Rs0.50 each. One household reported that a bag lasts about three days, and another that it gets through about four bags a week. Bags are either collected and carried home individually, which takes about three hours a week, or are collected on a more occasional basis and transported by lorry, at a cost of Rs10 for a month's supply. Total fuel costs, as such, remained much lower than for those purchasing firewood, although users have to buy special sawdust stoves, and probably have to replace cooking utensils more frequently as a result of the intense and concentrated heat which this kind of fuel produces.

For those households whose home gardens are sufficient to satisfy at least a part of their requirements, the ways in which fuel is obtained correspond closely to those already described in other communities. There are also a number of other less commonly used sources. Bean cultivators use *apala* sticks as frames, which are then used as fuel at the end of the season. All vegetables growers have to cut back hedges and prune trees about four times a year, and the wastes produced can also be used as fuel. The normal procedure, in both of these instances, is for hired labour to be engaged to cut and transport the wood. Finally, a small number of households has started to use paddy husks as fuel, although this, like sawdust, requires the use of a special type of stove.

Conclusion

Taking the six communities as a whole, the initial impression is one of great diversity.

Fuel is obtained from many different places, and individual sources may be exploited in various ways. Collection can sometimes be carried out in the course of other activities, which entails little or no additional time, and the initial stages of processing are often accomplished in the performance of tasks which would have had to be carried out irrespective of the need for fuel. In other instances, however, fuel-related activities are quite distinct from other work, and may entail opportunity costs.

Individual households combine the possibilities open to them in ways which reflect their particular circumstances. Some do not rely very much on collected fuel at all, but purchase most of their requirements. This diversity makes it difficult to quantify and compare the costs incurred in different places by different groups. It is, however, still possible to attempt a broad classification of the experiences which have been reviewed.

The first and largest category comprises those for whom the opportunity costs of the time devoted to fuel-related activities appear small. This includes all households which rely mainly on their own or other people's home gardens, since they are able to devote either small amounts of time throughout the year, which can be fitted in around other work, or longer stretches in periods when there is little else to do. This covers nearly everyone in Kandy, and between a quarter and a half of all cases in Badulla, a disproportionate number of whom are from the richer groups. It also includes those who gather fuelwood off-season from Crown or other privately owned upland in Nugathalawa and Sapugasdowa.

The second category encompasses those who incur significant opportunity costs. This is mainly made up of households collecting from tea estates, which have no option other than to expend substantial amounts of time during periods when income-earning opportunities are available. This covers most middle and poor households in Kanawarella, and most rich and middle households in Sapugasdowa. It also includes the much smaller group which is obliged to travel considerable distances to collect fuel regularly from Crown Land in these two communitites.

Third, there are those who must purchase fuel, who are concentrated in Nugathalawa especially among the poorer households.

On the basis of the evidence presented, it may therefore be concluded that most households currently encounter little difficulty in obtaining the fuel which they require, but that there is a significant minority for whom this may not be the case. The number of households in this category is likely to increase as time passes. As population grows, home garden size will diminish, and the proportion of households which is able to obtain fuel from land under its own control will diminish. At the same time, currently observable trends suggest that alternative sources, to which such households are currently able to turn, will themselves become more difficult to tap in future.

A comparison of Tables 4.2 and 4.3 indicates a predictable decline in access to other people's home gardens as average garden size diminishes, and it seems likely that very little fuel will be available from this source anywhere in a few years time. A number of households in Kandy reported that access to Crown Land was becoming more restricted, and although the particular factors responsible in this case were rather unusual, it would not be surprising if a similar trend were to become apparent elsewhere in years to come. In Sapugasdowa, estate management was reported to have recently banned the collection of tea clippings, so that these could be dug back into the ground to enhance soil fertility, and whilst this decision has yet to be enforced, further access to this source is now placed in doubt. The recent history of Nugathalawa provides a particular instance of land being taken out of tea production altogether and put to alternative uses which diminish fuel availability.

Competition for fuel from external and industrial sources is another factor with a possible bearing on future supplies, although this could also create new income-earning opportunities for some rural households. In Kandy, there is already a history of coconut husks being transported from the area studied for sale in the urban market, and although this trade was disrupted when the indirect route to Kandy was cut off by the reservoir, there are now signs that it will be revived as urban demand grows, and sources are sought from increasingly far afield. In Kandy, there is also the more local demand for fuel created by the tobacco industry, which was responsible for the removal of much of the original tree cover. Although nearly all fuel is currently brought in by the tobacco company, pressure on their current sources could lead to renewed attempts to exploit local sources in future.

All this suggests the likelihood that fuel availability, whilst a rather low priority at present, could increase in importance as time goes by. The chapters which follow describe and assess the activities which are currently being pursued to deal with this eventuality.

Notes

1. These were all sites selected by the CFP for farmers' woodlots. The reasons why they were chosen for the purposes of this particular piece of research will be discussed after the project itself has been introduced in Chapter 5.
2. See Soil Survey Unit, National Planning Division, 1984.
3. Apparently oblivious to what their colleagues in other ministries were

intending, the FD actually attempted to establish some farmers' woodlots on a part of this land. We had originally intended that the group involved should be included in our study, but the people of the colony, already antagonized by the way in which they had been treated, regarded our investigation as another unwelcome intrusion into their lives. The attempt was therefore abandoned at an early stage.

4. A number of factors have combined recently to make tobacco cultivation less attractive than was formerly the case. The area under cultivation has been reduced by some land being lost to the reservoir, and a further portion has been eliminated by government restrictions imposed to guard against soil erosion. Crop prices have failed to keep pace with those of critical inputs, and labour has become more difficult to find, as a result of competition from construction activities associated with the dam. For all this, tobacco remains a key element in the local economy and an important means of accumulation.

5. See Table 4.1. Kurundumulla is the exception. This is a very small community made up mainly of self-sufficient farmers, most of whom were members of the CFP. In contrast with the other communities in which groups were established, it was therefore not possible, in this instance, to incorporate non-members in the preliminary census and other surveys. The procedures for selecting informants are discussed in more detail in Appendix 1.

6. The figure reported by the household in our initial census was rather lower than this, which is reflected in the results presented in Table 4.3.

7. The totally landless accounted for 7 per cent of the population according to information supplied by one local offical.

8. See Gamage (1987).

SECTION III
THE INTERVENTIONS REVIEWED

5. The promotion of farmers' woodlots under the Community Forestry Project (CFP)

This chapter examines the CFP, which is the larger of the two major biomass energy-related interventions with which the Government of Sri Lanka has been associated. The account begins with an overview of the project as a whole, but then quickly focuses upon the key farmers' woodlot component.

Starting with a statement of how this was intended to proceed, and with a series of indicators which suggest a wide divergence between initial goals and achievements, the chapter then goes on to review the factors contributing to performance, and to explore the underlying reasons for the problems which were encountered.

The project in outline

The CFP started in 1982. It had a budget of US$13.7 million, of which US$10 million was to be provided as a loan by the ADB (Asian Development Bank), with the remainder coming from the Government of Sri Lanka. It was to last for six years, and to terminate at the end of 1987.

Rationale
The stated justification for the project rested on three sets of ideas, which enjoyed wide currency in international development circles in the late 1970s and early 1980s. The first

was the second energy crisis, which was apparently confirmed by the 1981 FAO study, and which placed Sri Lanka in the fuelwood deficit category. The second was the growing recognition of the environmental problems caused by deforestation, and the belief that fuelwood extraction was a contributory factor. And the third was the change in emphasis in forestry away from large-scale plantations towards smaller-scale systems, which could be controlled by rural people themselves, and used to satisfy their own immediate cash and subsistence needs.[1]

Against this background, the project sought, first: '. . . to use the local resources of the community; . . . to plant fuelwood on state land and help resolve the scarcity problem . . .' and second: '. . . to set the stage for a much larger planting programme by creating community awareness, and by building up required institutional support'. Work was to be concentrated in one Dry Zone and four Hill Country districts.

Components

Three major sets of activities were planned. The first involved the establishment of individual farmers' woodlots. These were to be of between a half and one hectare in size, and were to be located in small clusters in 90 different communities. Second, a single 25ha community woodlot was to be planted in each of the five districts. These were to be sited where there were Rural Development Societies which were prepared to take charge, and were to serve as experiments in the feasibility of collective control. Third, demonstration woodlots would be set up in each of the four Wet Zone districts with the purpose of publicizing planting, maintenance and other agro-forestry practices, creating community awareness of agro-forestry and providing centres for farmer training. In addition, there was to be a Community Forestry Research Unit in Badulla, with a Central Research Nursery, which would provide a number of technical support functions for the project as a whole.

Taken together, these activities were supposed to comprise the core of the real community forestry activities; yet between them they commanded only 8 per cent of the original budget (see Table 5.1) The larger part of what remained was to be devoted to 14000ha of block fuelwood plantations, which would be planted in Badulla, and run

74

Table 5.1: Percentages of budget allocated to different activities under the community forestry budget

	Original allocation[1]	Revision[2]
Field unit and woodlots[3]	7.5	3.7
Block fuelwood plantation	53.8	52.4
Research	1.2	0.7
Training overseas	4.5	1.6
Consultants	4.4	5.0
Local expenditures[4]	10.2	1.1
Unallocated	18.3	35.5
Total	100.0	100.0

1. Mid-term Review, 1987, p.40.
2. Revised estimates for 1982–9, Mid-term Review, p.42.
3. Includes farmers', demonstration and community woodlots.
4. Comprises civil works and in-country training.

along conventional lines by the FD. These would be supported by six nurseries, 169km of plantation roads and other facilities, including vehicles, housing and fire-fighting equipment, and would altogether absorb 54 per cent of the available resources.

Although having little to do with community forestry as such, this was justified on the grounds that the core of the programme was innovative, and high risk, and could not be expected to produce results within a time scale which would be consistent with the size of the problem confronted. As such, the plantations were seen as an interim solution, which would help to address fuelwood shortages during the period which it would take for the other components to come on stream.

The rest of the budget was accounted for by 75 man-months of consulting services, 118 months of overseas training fellowships, and a modest amount of in-country training.

The project was to be administered by a new Community Forestry Division within the Forest Department, with a field unit at Badulla, headed by a Deputy Conservator of Forests. A structure of committees would be appointed at the national, district and village levels in order to incorporate other agencies and interested parties into the processes of selecting participants and deciding about other aspects of project activity.

Table 5.2: CFP percentage of original staffing targets achieved 1982–86

Staffing area	Percentage
Block fuelwood plantation	75
Community forestry division[1]	35
Research unit	14
Overall	52

Source: Mid-term Review, pp. 24–5
1. The review proposed that an additional 24 posts should be created to enable the division to carry out its work properly. If these are added to the original target, attainment falls to 25 per cent.

The initial design of the farmers' woodlots component

Project documentation itself makes it clear that the block fuelwood plantations would always be too expensive to provide a viable long-term solution to any problem of fuel shortage which might arise, and these will therefore only be discussed in so far as they served to exert an influence upon other potentially more significant activities.

Attempts to set up village woodlots were almost completely unsuccessful, since hardly any functioning rural development societies could be found. Demonstration woodlots, by contrast, were established; but only comprised pure eucalyptus stands, and appear to have attracted little public interest. The research programme, whilst producing a series of potentially interesting, fuelwood-centred cropping patterns, has been confined almost exclusively to its own station, and has thus far received very little exposure to project participants.

From amongst the activities which the project has pursued, only the experience of the farmers' woodlots can help to throw light upon the central question with which we are concerned. The rest of the chapter will therefore concentrate almost exclusively upon this aspect.

Selection of districts
In the original project design, woodlots were to be established in Batticaloa in the Dry Zone, and in the Hill Country districts of Badulla, Kandy, Nuwara Eliya and Matale. Initial documents offered a range of reasons for selecting these locations.These are summarized in Table 5.3.

76

Table 5.3: CFP: reasons given for the selection of districts

	Badulla	Kandy	N'Eliya	Matale	B'caloa
Watershed protection needed persistent fuelwood deficit	x	x	x	x	
Local fuelwood prices high	x	x	x	x	
Large urban population		x			
Concentration of fuelwood using industries		x	x		
Site of major fuelwood market	x				
Low rural incomes/lack of facilities	x				x
Availability of suitable land	x	x	x	x	x

Selection of sites and participants

The project appraisal document envisaged a two-tiered administrative structure for the selection of sites and of farmers from within the chosen districts.

The process was to be set in motion with the establishment of Village Forest Committees, which would comprise the representatives of existing Rural Development Societies. These bodies would then put forward the names of potential participants to district-level committees, made up of various officials and a representative of the project. The district committees would then make the final decisions, and would subsequently assist in the various formalities involved in the allocation of land to successful applicants. These procedures were later revised to bring them into line with those normally employed for the acquisition of land by the FD. Under the modified system, it was intended that project staff should first agree that a particular piece of land was available with the Grama Sevaka and the AGA of the area in which it was located, and that the district Government Agent would then approve their decision. Next, the AGA would prepare a formal report on the land, and send it to the Commissioner of Lands for approval of its release for reforestation.

The District Superintendent of Surveys would then initiate a perimeter and plot survey, with stones being placed along the boundary, and a plan prepared for inclusion in official map records. Next, any land ownership disputes would be dealt with through the settlement officer. With these resolved, the project could then secure legal title to the land by gazetting it as forest reserve under the Forest Ordinance.

In deciding which sites should be put forward in this way, two main criteria were to be employed: they were to be in areas where there were fuelwood shortages and markets; and suitable Crown Land or Land Reform Commission land should be available. At a later stage, it was also decided that sites should, ideally, adjoin roads, in order to maximize their demonstration effect, although no reference to this appears in the original plan. Individual participants were to be required to have lived in the area for at least three years, and not to be government employees. Preference was to be given to small farmers.

Title to land

Within three months of being allocated plots, participants were to receive leases. These would be renewed annually for the first three years, subject to the satisfactory completion of work. After this, a six-year extension would be granted, followed by two further eight-year extensions, making a total of 25 years in all. Formally, the land would then revert to the government, although project officers indicated subsequently that a further 25-year lease would be a possibility.

Plot design

Precise details of how individual plots of land were to be organized were spelt out in the appraisal document. Eighty per cent of the area was to be devoted to *Eucalyptus grandis* and other fuelwood species, selected for their fast-growing properties, and planted in $30 \times 30 \times 30$cm holes at 3×2 intervals. The remainder was to be divided equally between eucalyptus, at wider 5×5m intervals, for pole production, and jackfruit at 10×10m intervals. The plot would be surrounded by a live hedge of *Gliricidia* or *Erythrina*.

Provision of labour and inputs

The work of land preparation, planting and protecting the trees would be the responsibility of the families taking part. They would also have to provide any tools which were required, and to obtain their own fertilizer, although it was assumed that this would be available from subsidized sources.

For its own part, the project undertook to supply seedlings, but not cuttings for hedges. To ensure good initial growth of trees, farmers would be required to weed four times in the year of planting, and twice in the following year, to a radius of half a metre around each plant. They would be allowed to grow crops between the trees in the early years where the terrain was suitable for this purpose.

Harvesting and disposal of produce

It was assumed that the plots would produce fuelwood in the seventh year, and thereafter every sixth year, until the 25th year, together with a more limited amount of pole timber. In addition, there would be some construction timber from *jak* trees in the 25th year, and cashew nuts and jackfruit once the trees had reached maturity. Fuelwood yields were expected to vary from 12 to 15 cubic metres per hectare according to species, location and rotation period.

Despite the prominence given, in initial statements, to the need to produce fuel to deal with rural shortages, it was assumed, in more detailed discussion later in the report, that 80 per cent of fuelwood would be available for sale to urban fuelwood centres, and that fruits would be marketed through private traders. For the project as a whole (that is, including the block fuelwood and other elements), it was calculated that an internal rate of return of 18.8 per cent could be achieved. This was described as a relatively modest figure, which could be justified in terms of the experimental nature of the activities involved.

A preliminary assessment of the woodlots component

Criteria

Four sets of criteria will be used in assessing the performance of the woodlots:

○ the extent to which physical targets are achieved;

○ the extent to which the benefits arising accrue to the poorer households who were targeted, and who were identified in Chapter 4 as being most likely to be affected by fuel shortages;

○ the likelihood of the woodlots being sustained after the withdrawal of project support;

○ the extent to which the environment has been protected.

Methods

Most of the evidence to be used in assessing performance derives from woodlots established in the six communities described in Chapter 4, all of which were studied in depth. It is important to recognize that these were not representative of the general experience of the project, but were purposively selected from among the small number of locations where records indicated significant levels of activity. Shorter visits were also made to nearly all of the other relatively successful groups, as well as to one or two of those where little appeared to have happened. Findings from these more impressionistic investigations are used to supplement those from the central studies, where appropriate. The methods of data collection employed are described in more detail in Appendix 1.

Data were also obtained from the project's own baseline study, which was conducted in 1984,[2] from the report of the mid-term review team,[3] which visited Sri Lanka in 1987, and from other records which were made available for our inspection.

Indicators

When the position was reviewed in 1987, a series of indicators derived from these sources, and from our own investigations, all pointed to the conclusion that the woodlots component was experiencing serious difficulties:

○ compared with a target area of 4055ha, only 178ha (or 4.4 per cent of the total) had actually been planted by the end of the year;

○ of the households allocated land under the project, the number who had actually planted only exceeded 50 per cent in the case of one of the communities studied;

○ according to project records only 3.2 per cent of the target area was planted successfully, that is with a seedling survival rate of 80 per cent or more at the end of the first year, and our own research suggested an even lower figure;

○ only 35 per cent of the intended complement of staff had been recruited by 1986, and most of those appointed were at a very junior level;

○ according to the mid-term review, by the end of the

80

intended project period, the woodlots would only have been able to absorb approximately half of the resources made available to them (see Table 5.1).

Within this overall context of under-performance, our own enquiries revealed that the woodlots had proved particularly unsuccessful in involving poorer households. Nearly all of the instances of flourishing and viable plots encountered were under the control of farmers commanding far higher than average levels of resources.

These findings, were, by themselves, sufficient to cause serious doubts about the sustainability of a community-based woodfuel planting programme and, on balance, this impression was confirmed by other evidence. A particularly striking finding was that less than half of the participants interviewed actually appeared to be aware that fuelwood production was the central objective. In addition, a considerable amount of evidence will subsequently be presented to suggest that the project served to undermine trust between households, thus reducing the prospects for the co-operation required for long-term success.

As regards the capacity of the project, either directly or indirectly, to contribute to environmental conservation, the evidence is not very clear-cut, but it appears rather doubtful that a significant positive effect could have been achieved.

The role of external factors

In seeking to understand why things went wrong, a wide range of factors must be taken into account. Some were entirely beyond the control of the projects, others derived from the competition for resources within it, especially with the block fuelwood plantations. These external factors must be dealt with first before turning to the subsequent analysis.

Factors beyond the project's control

Factors which the project could not control, and which could not reasonably have been foreseen at its inception, clearly go some way towards providing an explanation for the relative lack of success.

The civil disturbances, arising in Sri Lanka's eastern region in the early 1980s, prevented any work on farmers' woodlots from going ahead in Batticaloa District, where 56 per cent of the planting initially targeted for this part of the project was to have taken place. For the same reason, the forestry training school at China Bay in Trincomalee was unable to function, further complicating the already difficult process of in-country training of staff. The general situation obtaining in the country, and the demands placed by civil disturbances upon the public purse, almost certainly contributed to the failure of the government to provide a substantial portion of the US$3.7 million to which it was committed in the initial plans. Finally, it seems likely that unrest sometimes served to undermine the sense of security which people require before embarking upon a course of action which only promises returns in the comparatively long term. For understandable reasons, this factor appears likely to have been particularly influential in the case of Tamil households.

The second major external problem to be encountered was drought, with 62 per cent of households interviewed reporting that they were adversely affected to some extent. This was a problem throughout the period 1984–7, and was particularly severe in 1986 when all of the new seedlings which were planted died in some of the communities.

The Kandy villages, with their lower average rainfall, were more seriously affected, whilst within individual communities the impact was felt most by those who had stony land, or whose plots were in remote locations where it was difficult to carry water to seedlings during dry periods.

Competition for resources within the project
The second major set of factors undermining the progress of the woodlots was the competition for resources from other parts of the project. Although the project was supposed primarily to be designed to create the preconditions for widespread woodfuel tree cultivation by rural people themselves, the allocation of resources laid down in the initial plans suggested that the implicit priority was to maximize fuelwood production in the shorter term, using centrally managed plantation systems. This suited the project staff, who were familiar with such ways of working. It also suited the funding agency, in so far as a project of this type fitted far more readily within their established appraisal and lending procedures, than one with more diffuse, less readily quantifiable, training and institution-building objectives.

Once the project got under way, this initial bias against the woodlots was exacerbated by problems encountered in the plantations themselves. Foreshadowing issues which were to arise again in slightly different forms with the woodlots, difficulties were encountered in obtaining land, in supplying seedlings to sites, in establishing the technically demanding exotic eucalyptus species, in maintaining adequate standards of weeding in the face of unrealistically high target planting figures and with termite infestation.

With the block fuelwood component clearly established as the flagship, by which overall perceptions of performance would be shaped, the understandable reactions of staff was to concentrate their efforts on this part of the project, and to neglect other work. The extent of this effect is made clear by Tables 5.1 and 5.2, which show that both the proportion of initial budgetary allocations actually taken up, and of intended staff actually recruited, were both substantially greater in the block fuelwood component than with the woodlots.

The imbalance in favour of short-term production, and against longer-term institution-building objectives, was finally made even more pronounced by the programme of overseas training. This focused heavily upon the more technical aspects of forestry, and made little provision for the study of its wider human dimensions, thus depriving the junior staff, assigned to work on the community part of the project, of more senior specialist support.

Whilst it would have been necessary for these negative external factors to have been absent for the project to have attained its objectives, their elimination, by itself, would have been far from sufficient as a condition of success. As such, they should not be allowed to obscure the more fundamental deficiencies in project design, to which we may now turn. These will be considered in broadly chronological order, starting from preparatory activities, and then moving on to the implementation phase.

The land allocation process

The initial discussion of performance suggested two broad types of problem: those associated with getting people to plant trees, and those connected with the survival of seedlings, once in the ground. Difficulties arising in the selection and allocation of land were to prove especially influential as far as the former were concerned.

In some instances, problems could be attributed to the inability of project staff to follow the procedures initially envisaged. In others, defects inherent to the procedures themselves seemed to be responsible. The net effect was for members of certain groups to be deterred from taking part, and for others to participate for reasons which had little to do with the purposes for which the project was ostensibly designed. The manner in which issues of land allocation were handled also served, in a number of instances, to lay foundations for problems which were only to become fully apparent at a later stage in the evolution of the project.

The selection of sites

The story begins with the selection of sites, which took place in a manner which was quite different from what had originally been intended. There were a number of reasons for this, many of which were particular to individual locations.

To start with, the principle that the project should automatically be a party to initial decisions about sites and participants was only established in practice in 1986, after most of the groups presently in existence had already been set up. Prior to that, the project had only generally been represented in the case of groups in Badulla District, and even in these instances had not always participated as an equal partner.

The first consequence of this was that most of the criteria intended to govern the selection of sites were never taken very seriously. Neither the fuelwood situation, nor the proximity of sites to roads, appears to have exercised much influence. Some of the sites chosen do appear to have been fairly suitable, for example, in the Kandy research villages and in Nugathalawa, but this seems largely to have been a matter of chance, with areas of similarly high demand elsewhere being excluded, and many places where there was little evidence of shortages being chosen. A further problem was that many of the locations selected were far from ideal for forestry. On top of all of this, it also seems that little or no attempt was generally made to gauge how willing local people were to participate before decisions were made to go ahead.

Selection appears, rather, to have become a function of the personal agendas of the local officials involved, with the project being used as a vehicle to pursue objectives which were often far removed from those in terms of which it was initially conceived. In certain cases, like Kettiganawela and Ihaketiya, it provided an opportunity to dispossess political rivals where supporters of the previous government had been granted land. In others, such as Nugathalawa, it provided the possibility of tidying up complicated situations arising in the wake of successive waves of encroachment upon Crown Lands. The outcome was that project staff were left to deal with a diversity of situations, each carrying its own particular complications.

At the most basic level, they were confronted by many different types of physical environment. At one extreme, the sites provided were so rocky and steep that they were totally unsuitable. Others would have required a great deal of preparation, and still not have been suitable for the cultivation of inter-crops in the early years, which was required as a financial incentive to participants and as a means of ensuring a high standard of weeding. In addition, sites of this kind would often be relatively remote, and difficult to supervise, which increased the danger of trees being destroyed by fires from adjoining *chena* cultivation, or being trampled by grazing animals.

At the other end of the spectrum, some very good quality land was made available, posing the very different problem of selection from large numbers of applicants, and of promoting tree cultivation where participants would sooner have grown crops on a permanent basis.

Superimposed upon these initial differences were a variety of existing land uses and tenurial arrangements. In some instances these were to prove relatively unproblematic. At Kanawarella, for instance, all of the land to be allocated had previously been used by one individual to grow a low-value crop of *mara* grass, and had originally been obtained under an informal arrangement with the previous government; with no legal title, there was little that this person could do to resist the reallocation of the area.

In other places, like Allawataketiya, encroachers growing vegetables or tobacco, even when in possession of annually renewable *badu* leases, generally recognized the right of the government to reallocate the land as it saw fit, although the presence of relatively large numbers of small cultivators made things rather more difficult than in the previous instance.

Greater potential complications started to arise in cases where more permanent rights had previously been established or assumed. In Kettiganawela, on land which had again been used to grow vegetables, existing cultivators believed that they had the option to go on renewing their leases for a period of up to 99 years. In Dodangolla, the land selected immediately adjoined villagers' homes, and had generally been under continuous home garden cultivation, with farmers, in many instances, paying taxes of a type normally only levied on full *sina kara* land. In the extreme case of Perawella, which was not included in the main survey, land on which a great deal of labour had already been expended in the construction of terraces and other land improvements by one group of people was chosen, and then reallocated to another.[4]

The selection of participants

A variety of procedures for allocating plots to individuals were then superimposed upon these different pre-existing patterns of land use to create a still more complicated picture.

The procedure employed would generally start with bills being posted in the communities involved, which notified villagers that a land *kachcheri* would be held, and invited them to put their names forward. Isolated complaints indicated that this was not always done in an entirely straightforward manner, but the number of people prevented, by lack of information, from applying, does not appear to have been very great.

As with the initial identification of sites, the selection procedures which followed were, more often than not, conducted by local officials, without any involvement by project staff, and once again, original intentions were frequently lost sight of in the process. A circular was issued explaining selection criteria to the relevant bodies in 1986 but, as with other provisions, this was rather too late to have much effect, and seems likely, in any case, to have been disregarded.

In a small minority of cases, of which Nugathalawa was the most clear-cut example, the original idea of favouring small farmers was directly reversed. Here, the possession of non-agricultural income was made a condition of joining, on the grounds that those with greater resources at their disposal would not require much support in obtaining the required inputs of labour, and would be more likely to achieve high success rates.

This reasoning was to be justified by subsequent events, although its effect was to concentrate the control of much of the land in the hands of traders, who did not cultivate it themselves but instead relied upon hired labourers.

At the other extreme, an attempt was made to adhere to the original procedures in Nuwara Eliya, where only those with an income of less than Rs750 a month were considered. In most other cases, no formal attempts to employ a wealth-based criterion were made, although the frequent intrusion of political considerations into the selection process had the effect of biasing access in favour of the better off, as subsequently became apparent.

The degree of political interference varied significantly from one case to another, the scope for it being far greater where sites were considered desirable, and where the number of applicants exceeded the units available by a wide margin. It was most apparent at Kanawarella where, if local accounts are to be believed, the Grama Sevaka responsible for putting forward the name of the community was also the largest land owner within it. This individual was said to have had a direct interest in extending his existing forestry land to supply his sawmill business, and to have seen the project as a means of depriving a rival SLFP supporter of control of some land at the same time. It was suggested that members of the minority drummer and blacksmith castes had been entirely excluded, and that the only dominant caste members who had received allocations were close relations and political supporters of the chairman himself.

Elsewhere, opponents of dominant groups, and others not closely associated with them, were generally discriminated against to lesser degrees. In a few cases, however, access appears to have been far more open. In Sapugasdowa, a relatively poor and economically undifferentiated community, members of minority caste and ethnic groups enjoyed reasonable access, and much the same seems to have applied in Bambagala.

The allocation of plots

With the basic list of names agreed, specific pieces of land then had to be allocated to particular applicants. The procedures employed for this purpose varied from place to place.

The impersonal device of drawing lots was used in a number of instances. This worked reasonably well where land had not previously served any very important purpose, but was much less satisfactory where regular cultivation had already been taking place.

At Dodangolla, the authorities were prepared to recognize the difficulties which this caused when applicants approached them, and reallocated much of the land to former users. In Sapugasdowa, requests to change initial allocations so that people would not have to travel so far to their plots were also dealt with sympathetically.

At Kurundumulla, by contrast, less flexibility was shown, and although former users were all granted land, problems arose because many of the new allocated plots were further from individual homesteads than those previously cultivated, and thus less convenient to work. Farmers also complained that earlier labour-pooling arrangements between close relations with contiguous plots were disrupted when they were allocated more widely dispersed pieces of land.

Similar appeals were ignored in Bombagala. As a result, fewer participants subsequently became active in the project than might otherwise have been the case, and some of those who were active, took part with less enthusiasam than they otherwise would have done.

More serious problems were to arise where local politicians exerted influence to get plots allocated to people with no previous claim to the land in question, and where former users saw their access diminished or eliminated as a result. Although the precise difficulties encountered under circumstances differed from one site to another, the invariable outcome was for the area planted, or successfully cultivated, to be reduced.

In the extreme case of the village not included in the main survey, former users had to endure the doubly frustrating experience of seeing the larger part of the land they had prepared taken away from them, and then neglected by the new allottees, who lacked the experience to put it to good use. In Kanawarella, occupants of adjoining pieces of land, who felt they had a prior claim to forestry plots, destroyed seedlings shortly after they had been planted. Similar problems were reported with former users in Nugathalawa.

In these and other places, it seems likely that the prospects of such actions being undertaken deterred some allottees from planting in the first place. It is also probable, in a number of other cases, that new recipients of land hesitated to make substantial investments of time and resources for fear that what had been granted to them by virtue of political allegiance could just as easily be taken away if the opposition were to return to power.

At Dodangolla, an isolated individual, who had not received his original plot under the new allocation, simply refused to move. He threatened violence against the new allottees, and this led, in turn, to the intervention of the police and to a heightening of tension within the community.

Land surveying

Already difficult situations were, in many cases, subsequently made worse by serious inadequacies in the conduct of land surveys. The experience of one group in Badulla, which was not included in the main survey, encapsulates most of the things which could go wrong here.

Initially 10 hectares were set aside for distribution, about half of which had previously ben encroached, with the rest remaining unused. In accordance with project guidelines, the initial understanding was that this area would be divided into half-acre plots. Applications were invited, some 50–60 people put their names forward, and from these, 20 were duly selected.

The surveyors then came to mark out the land, and decided that the encroached portion should be excluded. This meant that plots had to be reduced in size to a quarter of an acre each. Boundaries were delineated accordingly, but these were then only indicated to those present, and not actually marked with stones, which left many people unclear as to their exact location.

Those who started to clear the land first exploited this situation by extending their own plots. The problem was then compounded by a local officer who was said to have interfered with original allocations. In some instances, it was claimed that land was switched between original allottees. He was also accused of setting one piece of land aside for a cemetery when there was already one in the village, and then subsequently allowing another person to use it.

It was impossible, in the time available, to check these allegations, but even if incorrect, they are indicative of the suspicions and dislocation which can arise in politically divided communities, where clear procedures are not pursued. Whilst the powerful and confident are able to press forward regardless, others fear that the confusion will eventually lead to the need for a resurvey and new allocations, and thus hesitate to work the land which may rightfully be theirs.

This was a particularly bad case, but it would be unusual to encounter a group which had not experienced any of the kinds of difficulties documented here. At the same time, there were other cases which, in certain particulars, were actually worse than the instance which has been discussed. At Sapugasdowa, the surveyor's map, which no villager had seen until we showed it to them in the course of our research, bore no recognizable relation to the layout of plots on the ground. Even at Nugathalawa, the model group which visitors would generally be taken to see, it was reported that some boundary disputes had arisen.

Land tenure

The land survey bottleneck, together with unresolved questions about the types of land on which the project could and could not operate, and the rights of individuals which were left in its wake, was the major factor preventing the completion of the sequence of procedures required for the department to secure legal control over woodlot land. This, in turn, meant that the department lacked the legal authority to sign leases. None was issued at all before 1987.

Lack of legal title meant that participants were not eligible for inputs and assistance from other agencies, and could not receive tools from the FD itself. This helps to explain further difficulties arising in the implementation phase, which are discussed below.

Concerns about rights to land, or to the trees which would be grown on it, appear to have inhibited some people from applying for woodlots in the first place. Far more common, however, were those who were encouraged to put their names forward on the basis of unduly optimistic assumptions about their rights.

90

Misinformation and farmers' priorities

Enquiries revealed that most of those allocated land did not understand the nature of the conditions under which it was to be cultivated. Stated expectations varied, at one extreme, from those who thought that they were to receive full ownership rights, to those, at the other, who believed they would only be able to inter-cultivate with no rights, even to wood. Most people seemed to assume that they were to receive greater security of tenure than that which was actually to be allowed.

More fundamental still, were the misconceptions surrounding the purpose for which participants believed trees were to be grown. Many believed that watershed protection was the main goal, whilst others thought that it was timber production. Only in Nugathalawa, where an intensive effort to promote the woodlots was made, were a clear majority of participants aware of the fact that the project was primarily intended to produce fuelwood.

Misunderstanding extended further still in at least one village, where the 12 applicants did not even initially appreciate that they were supposed to grow trees. All dropped out at a later stage when the real objective was made clear to them.

Apart from reflecting on project organization, the widespread nature of these misunderstandings clearly also says something about the priority villagers attached to fuel production in relation to alternative land uses, a subject to which we will return later.

Many instances were also encountered of people who believed they would receive extensive aid in the form of cash, fertilizer, tools, and even guns for protection against wild animals. As the following discussion of initial costs makes clear, the prospect of such forms of assistance was particularly attractive to poorer households, and many later left the scheme on discovering they were not to be provided.

There can be little doubt that some of these misconceptions were deliberately fostered by the authorities involved as a means of creating interest. On other occasions, it seems that promises were made in the genuine expectation that assistance could actually be provided, over and above that which had been envisaged in the original plans. The project was, at that stage, exploring the possibility of help under the World Food Programme (WFP). Rights to certain inputs might also have become possible under programmes run by other agencies if individuals had been able to secure legal title to the new land more readily than actually proved to be possible. Finally, and especially in those cases where projects staff were not initially involved, it seems likely that officials themselves were genuinely unaware of the actual state of affairs.

Later developments were to show that many who were allocated land under these procedures failed subsequently to work it, and had only applied in the first place as a result of being quite unclear as to the nature of what it was they were applying for. Many applicants, on the other hand, whilst aware of the true nature of what was on offer, still put their names forward, even though they had little interest in fuelwood production as such.

Some who acted in this way were anxious to preserve or strengthen an existing claim on land which they were already cultivating, whilst others sought to establish such a claim with similar purposes in mind. Given a free hand, either group would have preferred the quick and regular returns offered by annual crops to the uncertain and deferred possibilities presented by trees. The strategy was to agree to engage in fuelwood production in the hope that they would at least be able to cultivate crops in the short run.

Trees were readily acceptable to the better off, who had a greater capacity to take a long-term view, as well as to those in areas where plots were too steep to permit crops to be grown. Even in these instances, however, there was still a pronounced tendency to reject the mono-cropping of fuelwood as a viable land-use strategy. Instead, people preferred multi-purpose species, which could offer a flow of benefits through time, or those which would eventually provide timber.

Although valued as a by-product, fuel for subsistance purposes was not seen as a particularly pressing need by most households, as will already be apparent from the account in Chapter 4. Neither were the prospects for commercial fuelwood production judged to be very attractive, when these were compared with alternative options for income generation.

This concludes the discussion of key developments in the decisive preliminary phase, which was largely the preserve of project staff and other officials. The account now moves on to the next stage, where farmers were to become more actively involved for the first time, and where a new set of problems was quickly to become apparent.

The allocation of costs

These problems derived from the various costs with which farmers were confronted. These fell into three broad categories: for nearly everybody involved, participation entailed at least an element of income foregone; it was usually necessary to hire a certain amount of labour; and various inputs had to be procured. Taken together, this required an outlay which, to many, appeared prohibitively high, given the period of time which would need to elapse before any returns could accrue. The difficulties encountered in the succeeding phase of implementation are considered in more detail below.

Land preparation

Land preparation would generally involve three stages: the removal of existing vegetation, the construction of 6m-wide ridges (each of which would accommodate two rows of trees) and the digging of holes for individual seedlings. The amount of labour required to perform these operations would vary, to some extent, according to the steepness of the land, but was mainly a function of whether the plots had previously been cultivated.

In the Kandy villages, where woodlots were sited on land which had formerly been used to grow vegetables, the amount of clearing required was limited, the area was already partially terraced, and an average of only 50 person days a hectare was needed. In the Badulla villages, on the other hand, where the levels of previous use were much lower, about twice the quantity of labour was required. This disparity was also reflected in the number of tools used. In some cases, one *mammoti*, purchased at a cost of approximately Rs100, was reported to have been sufficient. In others, two or three were necessary.

Most of the work could be carried out in the dry agricultural off-season when the opportunity cost of labour was comparatively low. On average, households were able to provide about half of the labour required themselves, with women and men contributing to roughly the same extent. In the socially homogenous communities of Kettiganawela and Kanawarella, most of the balance was provided through labour-exchange arrangements. Elsewhere, it was supplied predominantly by hired labour, nearly all of which was male. Taking the groups investigated as a whole, the average wage bill for a typical half-hectare plot was a little less than Rs600.

Together with the cost of tools, this represented a considerable outlay for many households, and was undoubtedly among the major factors contributing to the drop-out rate between land allocation and planting. This was especially the case with those who had applied under the misapprehension that various forms of support were to be provided.

Project staff realized from a fairly early stage that this would be a problem, particularly in less favoured locations. In the absence of any provision within their own budget, attempts were therefore made, from 1984 onwards, to arrange for assistance under the WFP. In 1987, it was claimed that agreement had finally been achieved, but by that stage it was already too late for the groups under investigation, as well as for a large proportion of the others in the programme.

Planting

The next operation was planting and, here again, the amount of time required varied considerably by location.

The first important variable was the distance, and the nature of the terrain which had to be traversed, in bringing seedlings and fertilizers from roadside to plot. The worst affected, from this point of view, were the farmers at Alawataketiya, who had to carry inputs for a kilometre over steeply sloping land, with no proper pathway, and those at Sapugasdowa who had to cover a rather greater distance over less difficult land.

The second was the density of planting. This tended to be greatest on the steepest land, where inter-cropping could not be practised (that is, at Kanawarella and Sapugasdowa), and least where the opportunities for inter-cropping were best (at Allawataketiya and Nugathalawa).

On average, farmers provided just over 50 person-days a hectare to this work, although this could be as little as 20 at one extreme, and over 100 at the other. The latter figure, however, covers a large element of replanting, which was made necessary in certain locations by drought and other problems discussed below. Although needing appreciably less time than land preparation, this work coincided with heavy demand for household labour for vegetable and tobacco cultivation in the Kandy communities, for paddy in Kanawarella and Sapugasdowa, and for a combination of the two in Nugathalawa. Very little exchange labour could therefore be arranged at this time of year, and participants had to rely upon hired labour for about a third of the total requirements.

In certain instances, meeting these requirements did not present serious difficulties. In Sapugasdowa, for example, neighbouring villages started paddy cultivation rather earlier, and were therefore available. Others were not so fortunate, and labour shortages at critical times help to explain why work was not done to the ideal standard in some cases, and why planting was sometimes not possible at all. Seasonal labour shortages also help to explain why nobody planted the boundary hedges proposed in the original plans, although a lack of extension advice may also have been partially responsible.

Weeding

With planting completed, the only major operation remaining was weeding. This was critical to the successful growth of the seedlings and, when done to the required standard, typically absorbed 90–100 person-days a hectare in the first year. As with planting, most households were unable to find all of this time themselves, and even though the work could be spread out over a longer period than other operations, an average of about a third of total requirements was once again hired.

Because the operation was so demanding of labour time, these ideal inputs only tended to be made in cases where suitable conditions for inter-cropping enabled people to secure a quick return. This, in turn, casts some doubt on the strategy of encouraging people to plant trees very close together so as to ensure the rapid shading out of weeds, in so far as this may sometimes have discouraged any weeding at all by making initial vegetable cultivation more difficult.

Fertilizer application

Project documents indicate the need for farmers to apply

fertilizer as a means of accelerating growth, and counteracting the danger of smothering by weeds in the early stages. The favoured practice involved the application of nitrogen, phosphorus and potassium prior to the first weeding, with a repetition a year later.

Although recommending this procedure, there was no provision, in initial plans, for fertilizer to be provided for farmers, since it was envisaged that farmers would secure their own supplies from what were described as subsidized sources. This seems to have been a reference to the Department of Minor Export Crops, but it was subsequently to transpire that this channel was only open to people who enjoyed full legal title to their land.

In the case of a few groups, who were apparently chosen on an ad hoc basis, the project helped by procuring and distributing its own supplies. Sometimes this appears to have worked smoothly, but on other occasions rivalries within villages appear to have led to a situation where some participants were excluded.

Elsewhere, some individuals made their own arrangements, often involving themselves in considerable expense in the process. One informant in Kandy reported that labour had to be hired to carry the bags from the store where they were purchased to the steep hillside location where they were to be used, whilst another had to sell jewellery to cover the cost of purchase. Faced with these kinds of difficulties, most households were simply left to manage, without being able to use any fertilizer at all.

Taken as a whole, such difficulties appear to have been felt most severely in the Kandy communities, where half of all households interviewed reported that they experienced some problem. In Badulla, the average proportion falling into this category dropped to 25 per cent, most probably reflecting the relative proximity of sites to the project headquarters.

Other constraints

The delivery system

The final factor contributing to low levels of planting in several locations was the failure of the project to deliver seedlings at the right time.

In order to flourish, seedlings need to be planted as soon as possible after the onset of continuous rains. In practice, for most of the project area, this left a fairly narrow window of opportunity early in the north-east monsoon, extending from late October to around the end of November, although in the parts of Kandy and Nuwara Eliya receiving the south-west monsoon, the opportunity also arose of planting in late May or June.

Often the delivery system proved unequal to these needs. In Kurundumulla, members claimed that seedlings were sent to them at a time when there was no rain at all although, in fairness, it should be pointed out that this was an area which was particulaly affected by drought. In Sapugasdowa, it was reported that land was prepared for planting in 1984, but that no seedlings were received at all until 1986, by which time the land had once again become overgrown. Villagers suspected that their close association with the opposition political party was the primary reason for the long delay.

Favouritism and political patronage were also believed to have led to the maldistribution of seedlings within communities. The most serious incident of this kind was reported in Kanawarella, where it was claimed that a dominant group controlled the process of allocation, withholding seedlings from some farmers who had already prepared their land, whilst distributing to others who were not even members. According to our informants, feelings ran high as a result, but the protest was eventually quashed, when those controlling allocation enlisted the help of the police to harass the organizers. This version of events is denied by those against whom the allegations have been made, who dismiss it as a typical symptom of the jealousy invoked in divided communities by projects of this type. A further problem encountered with the delivery of seedlings was that considerable numbers appear to have died during transportation to sites as a result of inadequate loading procedures.

Although possibly defective in each of these critical respects, one aspect of performance serves to present this part of the project in a more positive light. This was the flexibility shown by those in charge in responding to farmers' requests that the range of seedlings provided should be extended to include more multiple-use and non-fuelwood species, such as margosa and *tuna*.

Animal damage
Animal damage affected two-thirds of the households in the

97

survey. This general category covered a range of more specific problems. In two villages, but especially in Nugatha-lawa, rabbits and other wild animals eat young seedlings.

In two other cases, cattle eat *jak* seedlings. In addition, in nearly all villages, some damage was caused by cattle and buffaloes trampling over the recently planted land. It is impossible to distinguish those incidents which were accidental from those which were motivated by malice, but there appears to have been some correlation between the extent of damage, and the level of disputes relating to land allocation. The absence of fencing should also be taken into account as a contributory factor in all of the cases discussed.

The other type of damage arose from boar, monkeys, birds and other wild animals attacking inter-crops, which indirectly affected the viability of the trees by discouraging weeding. This was a problem everywhere, but was particularly severe in the Kandy villages, where animals had been driven into the immediate areas of the woodlots from their original habitats with the creation of the reservoir. The possibility that woodlots would, in future, themselves harbour wild animals which would attack crops, was itself regarded by some people as a disincentive to participation.

Termites

More than half of all households reported losing seedlings through termite attack. This affected young trees most and became more prevalent under drought conditions. The Kandy villages were the worst affected. One solution was to spray aldrin, where available, but this is highly toxic and is believed to have harmful health and environmental side effects. Another might have been to promote the use of less vulnerable indigenous species.

Extension

Project staff had little previous experience of extension, and this created difficulties in both phases of the project. At the outset, officers made themselves available to explain what was involved to participants, and farmers expressed no dissatisfaction as far as this aspect of the work was concerned. But, at a later stage, it appears that insufficient time was available to supervise operations.

Partly as a result, only a minority of participants followed the suggested spacing. Some chose to plant at a higher density, in the unfounded belief that this would increase yields and returns. Others opted for wider spacing, seeing this as a means of maximizing returns from inter-cropping in the early years, and of extending the period in which inter-cropping could be practised.

Staff also found difficulty in meeting the demands which arose as the project got under way. On the positive side, they did provide more seedlings for replanting where those initially supplied failed to establish themselves as a result of drought or other problems. As we have already seen, they were also able to help some farmers with fertilizers and pesticides. From other points of view, the picture was less satisfactory.

About a quarter of all farmers interviewed expressed dissatisfaction with the quality of the advice which they received. The species selected needed quite sophisticated silvicultural techniques if they were to flourish, but farmers' previous experience was generally limited to varieties which were either entirely self-propagating, or required only minimal maintenance. Several also commented that they lacked the necessary knowledge for fertilizer and pesticide applications, or for pruning and harvestings, and complained that the project made no provision for their instruction in these respects. Difficulties were again most pronounced in the Kandy area, where more problems requiring advice were encountered, and where contact with the project headquarters was less frequent. In extreme cases, participants claimed that they did not see the forestry officers at all after preparation and planting were completed.

The marketing and use of produce
At the time when data were being collected, no trees were mature enough to be harvested, and it is therefore only possible to speculate about what would have happened at this stage. There is, however, already evidence to suggest that even woodlots which currently appear successful may deteriorate over time, as poorer farmers seek in various ways to impair the growth of trees as they become larger, and start to shade out the inter-crops.

Even where this is not a problem, there are still questions about how readily permits will be forthcoming for felling, and about how trees can be felled and removed from some plots in the absence of pathways, without the simultaneous removal of trees from all surrounding land. Given the likelihood that only a small proportion of the wood produced will be required for local consumption, difficulties are also likely to arise in the transportation of wood from often quite remote and difficult sites to markets. Finally, there is the as-yet untested nature of those markets themselves.

Most farmers appear to believe that they will be able to produce wood or timber of at least pole quality, for which demand does exist, but the close spacing they have been advised to follow, and which they have often exceeded in the belief that this will lead to higher returns, will most probably mean that the product will only be suitable for fuelwood, and hence more difficult to sell.

Assessing performance

Economic returns
Even without these additional potential complications, and making due allowance for the large variations in performance which will arise between and within communities, it is already clear that the final results achieved will not be good. This is borne out by the findings of the project's own mid-term review, which suggested that the woodlot component would make a loss of US$0.7 million, and that a 50–75 per cent subsidy of all costs arising during the first two years would be required before farmers could anticipate the 13–20 per cent returns on their investments, deemed necessary to make participation attractive.

When some of the assumptions from which these results are derived are considered, even this appears to overstate actual performance. For example:

o Unskilled labour is priced at 35 per cent of its market value to allow for the fact that only a small amount of hiring is required. If the figures cited earlier are representative, this virtually amounts to assuming that the opportunity cost of unpaid household labour is zero.

o Land is valued at Rs500 a hectare to reflect its assumed value as grazing land. This should be regarded as a minimum figure, given the preponderance of more valuable alternative uses in practice.

o Fuelwood is valued at the price of kerosene, on the assumption that this represents its immediate substitute.

100

In practice, people nearly always substitute out of fuel-wood into lower-value fuels, such as crop residues. In this connection it should, however, be pointed out that the value of Rs2.15/litre used was only a third of that assumed for the 1982 appraisal, and that the effect of this error is therefore much less than was formerly the case.

o It is assumed that an unspecified proportion of the final product will be in the form of the higher-value timber, which farmers prefer to grow. Whilst it is true that this is what they prefer, there are strong grounds for supposing that close spacing will mean that only wood of sufficient quality for fuel will actually be produced.

Identifying winners and losers
In commenting on this analysis, it is at the same time important to recall that it does not reflect the range of different situations in which participants found themselves. Leaving aside differences arising from variations in the amount of labour required for land preparation, in the degree of exposure to drought and other problems, three distinct types of situation may be identified.

First, there were those households who were allocated land which had little previous use, and on which inter-cropping could not be practised. This was the most straightforward set of circumstances, and applied in the case of Kanawarella and parts of Sapugasdowa. In the first year, most participants falling within this category had to accept a substantial loss arising from the combined effects of hiring labour, purchasing tools, and other income-generating opportunities foregone. The extent of this deficit would have varied, in individual cases, from as little as Rs100 to as much as Rs1800, around an average of Rs800. Much smaller shortfalls would again have been encountered in years two and three, with weeding and vacancy filling, although some households would have been able to have carried out these tasks without incurring any financial cost. The situation would then have to return to its pre-project state for the next three years, until harvesting around year seven, when significant labour and material inputs would again be required, and the only return on all earlier investments would accrue. Assuming a reasonable final harvest, participants falling into this category would probably end up as overall winners.

The second general situation arose where those who were previously cultivating the land on which woodlots were sited continued to do so under the project. This applied to most cases in Kandy, and to about half in Nugathalawa, where participation could be interpreted as a defensive strategy, designed either to retain some claim on a valued resource, or to secure the opportunity to continue to cultivate vegetables and other crops during the period preceding shading out. In addition to the categories of costs arising in the previous example in the first year, farmers here would have had to have accepted an initial reduction in crop yields, which would have increased through years two and three, before the crop disappeared altogether around year four. Although part of the deficit might have been made good by using the labour released to generate new or additional income from other sources, it appears likely that participants in this group would become net overall losers. In the first year, Kandy farmers in this category generally ended up between Rs1000 and Rs2000 worse off, although for some the deficit was much larger. In Nugathalawa the shortfall was rather less, averaging about Rs400.

The third category comprised those for whom the project provided a means of access to new land on which cultivation was possible. This occurred to some extent in the Kandy villages, as well as in Nugathalawa. Whilst the costs encountered elsewhere would have applied once again in this case, they would have been counteracted by the additional returns from cultivation, with net gains sometimes even being achieved within the first year. Returns from vegetable and potato cultivation could be particularly high, even when allowance was made for the need, in certain instances, for labour to be diverted from home garden cultivation, and other previous income-generating activities. Net gains of Rs3000–4000 a year were common, and in extreme cases in Kandy households were more than Rs20000 a year better off. This group, therefore, emerges as the clearest net winner from the project at this stage, and there is little reason to suppose that this judgement will need to be revised when trees are eventually harvested.

Two additional points should, however, be borne in mind. The first is that the investment costs of breaking into the potato market in Nugathalawa were quite high, creating a situation where only the comparatively well-off were able to take the initial risk and reap the benefits. Second, alongside the category of winners, must be set those who previously cultivated the land in question, and who become the greatest net losers from the project as a whole.

Before moving on to a wider consideration of the equity implications of the project, it should furthermore be recalled that disadvantages would also have accrued to those who had been hired to work formerly cultivated land. Although generally better off in the first year, persons falling within this category could nearly all expect their employment opportunities to diminish through the second and third years, and to disappear altogether thereafter.

Finally, cross-cutting all of the other categories discussed, were the particular implications of the project for women. In general, these appear to have been less pronounced than might have been the case in other countries, were there is a more rigid gender division of labour, but two significant sets of consequences could still be identified. First, where women did not engage directly in the new form of production, additional labour was often hired or obtained through exchange arrangements, especially in the first year. The effect here was to increase the amount of work involved in food preparation, since meals would generally be provided in either instance. More often, however, women worked along-side men on the plots, providing an average of about a third of all labour, and only a little less than half of domestic inputs. As in the other case, the effect here was a net increase in the amount of work to be performed, although as field work increased there was a tendency for less essential domestic work to be cut back, or substituted through the purchase of pre-prepared foods.

There will also be some longer-term effects for women in the form of enhanced fuelwood availability, but this will only be of significance in the minority of cases where fuel-wood shortages are beginning to be encountered. As a post-script to this discussion, it is also interesting to note that woodlots had, in some cases, actually reduced short-run fuel availability by occupying land from which collection had previously taken place.

The participation of poorer households

As the last example demonstrates, the gains and disadvantages arising from the project were not distributed randomly between the different socio-economic groups of which participating communities were made up. In this section an attempt is made to draw together evidence from different stages in the project on the access enjoyed by different classes.

At the outset, there was some ambiguity as to who the primary beneficiaries were intended to be. Documents appeared to be advocating a focus on small farmers, although without going so far as to identify who they were supposed to be; but, in certain areas, this priority was reversed in the belief that this would lead to a higher degree of success. Out of this initial confusion arose a state of affairs where poorer households started at a slight disadvantage, which then became progressively more pronounced as events unfolded.

Initially, members of this group were less likely to receive information about the project. Publicity was generally controlled by village leaders, who sometimes chose only to inform the members of their own immediate circles.

Next, poorer households, and members of weaker ethnic and religious groups, were sometimes less inclined to submit applications, fearing that they would lack the political power to secure a fair return on any investment which they might be able to make; especially when the period elapsing between investment and return was so long. They were also most likely to be deterred by the complexities and uncertainties surrounding the access to land which was to be granted under the terms of the lease.

Those who did apply were able to bring influence to bear upon the selection and allocation processes, and were thus more likely to receive land. The cumulative effect of this, and of earlier factors, was that the poor, who comprised 45 per cent of all households, only accounted for 37 per cent of those initially given plots. At the same time, although we were unable to collect data on the subject, it appears probable that former users of woodlot sites, who were subsequently denied access, would have been drawn, to a disproportionate extent, from this group.

At the next stage, wealthier households had the resources needed to hire the labour and purchase the tools required to clear land for cultivation, whilst many poorer households did not, and were forced to drop out. This imbalance was exacerbated by deficiencies in the land-surveying process, which often allowed those who started first to extend the areas cultivated well beyond their notional allocations.

Even where poorer households were in a position to clear land and to start cultivating, they were often deterred from doing so by uncertainty regarding boundaries and future land rights. They lacked the confidence of their richer counterparts that they would be able to hold on to any land which they might have started to work. Dominant wealthier households were also able to capture a disproportionate share of the physical inputs supplied by the project, often denying access to others in the process. Where needed inputs were not made available, they were better placed to secure inputs and hire labour for themselves.

None of these obstacles was insurmountable, but in the absence of countervailing support from the project, each served to filter out a proportion of poorer households. The cumulative effect was that hardly any households in this category eventually became successful cultivators.

Given this tendency, it is no coincidence that the major success story was Nugathalawa, where the proportion of wealthy families was far larger than in any of the other communities. Elsewhere, it tended to be only a small minority of better-off households whose woodlots were able to flourish, and these, as we saw in the last chapter, were the people who were least in need of fuel.

Sustainability

The fact that the basic model proposed for woodlots was not economically viable for most households was, by itself, sufficient to undermine the prospects of sustainability. Other conditions necessary for the achievement of this end were also, for the most part, not met, although the picture was not entirely negative.

Although woodlots were organized so that rights and responsibilities were allocated to individual households, ultimate success required that people should, at least for certain purposes, function collectively. Initial terracing was much more effective if carried out across a hillside, rather than being confined to scattered plots. Participation required a

105

sense of security and trust in others, if people were to have the confidence to make an expensive investment, which would have to remain in the ground for several years before it could be harvested. Harvesting could not be carried out by households acting individually, but would require co-ordination for trees to be removed from sites after felling. These considerations highlight the significance of the institutional aspects of the project and, more specifically, the extent to which it served to reinforce or weaken intra-communal bonds.

On balance, as a result of difficulties discussed in earlier sections, the overall effect of the project in this respect has clearly been negative. New divisions have been created, and existing ones widened. In particular, friction has arisen between:

○ those receiving land, and unsuccessful applicants, especially where the latter were previous users;
○ those allocated land, and those able to appropriate it from them as a result of deficiencies in the way in which land surveying was conducted;
○ people who received land, but then were denied access to seedlings and other inputs, and those who encountered no difficulty in obtaining their requirements.

Working individually, or in combination with each other in different locations, these problems have led, at the very least, to passive resentment on the part of those excluded. In other cases, things have deteriorated further into various forms of covert resistance. Animals have been allowed to trample seedlings. More direct forms of destruction have been resorted to. Theft has taken place in certain instances. In extreme cases, open protest and attempts to retain or seize land by threats and force have been encountered.

There has, however, also sometimes been a more positive side to the picture. In the Kandy villages, people with plots who had not co-operated previously entered into exchange labour relations to prepare and weed their land, and to transport seedlings. In Sapugasdowa, there was co-operation between villagers who had previously only worked together on paddy cultivation, and labour was hired in from neighbouring villages for the first time. Almost everywhere, farmers took collective responsibility for scaring animals away from each others' plots, although no formal systems for guarding land were established. In Bambagala, an internal system of fertilizer loans was established to tide individuals through periods when they were unable to obtain their requirements. In the Kandy villages, Sinhalese participants, who in general had greater previous experience of tree cultiviation, advised less experienced Tamils, with whom they had little previous contact. In Nugathalawa, participants formed their own society with elected representatives to deal with project and other officials on their behalf.

Taken together, these examples suggest that potential does exist for communities to sustain forestry activities successfully where deficiencies of external management can be rectified.

Sustainability may also be seen as a function of farmers' ability to master new tree cultivation practices. Despite the choice of species which could not survive readily in local conditions, and which, as a result, afforded relatively few learning opportunities, our enquiries indicated that some strengthening of technological capability did still take place.

To determine the significance of this effect, participants were asked to report what they had learned through taking part, and responded with a wide range of ideas covering different aspects of the production process. Some of the more commonly made suggestions dealt with:

○ the criteria which should be taken into account in selecting species;

○ the spacing of plants and of terraces, including ideas derived from tea estate practices;

○ the retention of weeds and other materials from land clearance to make bunds across the slope;

○ the timing and technique of hole digging to get as much topsoil as possible, and the use of compost;

○ the optimum dimensions for holes, and means of preventing wind damage and aiding water retention;

○ the construction of fencing around individual trees to provide protection from animals;

○ the timing and frequency of fertilizer application, and methods to prevent it from being washed away;

107

○ the construction of drainage channels to aid water collection and prevent soil erosion.

Some of the suggestions made were judged, by project staff and other specialists, to reflect the inexperience of participants, and probably would not have been practical. For example, a proposal for small trenches to be constructed around trees to help retain water would, at the same time, have increased the danger of termite and fungus infestation. Others were already known and endorsed by project staff.

When both of these categories are allowed for, however, a number of ideas, which were both original and worthy of general consideration, remained. These included the new fertilizer application techniques. In other cases, a knowledge of particular local conditions helped farmers to put forward ideas which might not have been apparent to outsiders, such as the importance of selecting wind-resistant varieties in Nugathalawa. The question of how this potential might be exploited is taken up in Chapter 7.

Protection of the environment

The final criterion for assessing performance concerns the extent to which woodlots have contributed to the protection of the environment. Although project documents are not entirely clear on how this was to be achieved, two broad sets of possibilities seem to be implied. The first was that the provision of alternative sources of fuel would diminish the need for people to gather woodfuel from hillsides, and thus reduce levels of soil erosion. The second was that planting woodlots on previously denuded hillsides could have the same effect.

Neither of these propositions stands up well to investigation. Providing alternative sources of fuel would have little effect, since, as we saw in Chapter 4, few people currently satisfy their fuel needs by gathering from hill locations, and those who do would hardly ever cut down live trees. At the same time, planting for fuelwood would not provide protection, since the initial clearing of the land, and the subsequent periodic felling of trees, would tend to increase rather than diminish existing levels of soil erosion.

Whilst revealing some redeeming features, the detailed account of the course of the woodlots component of the project, and of its performance against central criteria provides broad confirmation of the negative assessment offered at the outset. The concluding sections of the chapter have indicated how things went wrong. The underlying causes of the difficulties encountered are explored in the first section of Chapter 7, after the discussion of the other major intervention which now follows.

Notes

1. Foley and Barnard (1984).
2. Gamage (1987).
3. Asian Development Bank (1987).
4. In contrast to what has been found elsewhere, tree, as opposed to land, tenure does not appear to have been an issue here, for the simple reason that very few trees remained on the selected sites.

6. The promotion of domestic cooking stoves under the National Fuelwood Conservation Programme (NFCP)

This chapter explores the attempt to promote the use of improved domestic cooking under the National Fuelwood Conservation Programme (NFCP), which was the second major biomass energy-related initiative to be undertaken by the Sri Lankan Government. The discussion begins with a brief review of the international experience of stoves programmes, and goes on to examine the factors which have traditionally influenced the choice of stove design in Sri Lanka. The process leading to the design of the new stove is then described, and the nature of the NFCP is outlined. This leads on to the major part of the chapter, in which the private and social benefits claimed for the programme are assessed. A brief concluding section then outlines an alternative approach to stove promotion, which has been pursued by the government during the period since the completion of the fieldwork upon which most of the book is based.

The international setting
Isolated attempts to encourage people to adopt improved domestic cooking stoves may be traced back at least as far as the 1940s,[1] but it was not until the identification of the 'other energy crisis', and the related environmental concerns arising in the late 1970s, that stove programmes began to receive serious attention. Research conducted at this time suggested that large numbers of households were using very basic three-stone designs which wasted between 90 and 95

per cent of all the heat generated. Relatively simple alternatives, by contrast, proved capable of reducing losses to around 70 per cent under laboratory conditions, thus apparently holding out the prospect of savings of the order of 70–80 per cent of total consumption.[2]

Encouraged by this potential, about 100 programmes had been initiated by 1983,[3] leading to the distribution of approximately 100000 stoves worldwide.[4] A number of different countries in Africa, Asia and Latin America were involved, with Guatemala, Kenya, Senegal, Indonesia and India in the forefront. Although varying in emphasis from one place to another, these initiatives exhibited many common features.[5] They were organized almost exclusively around the objective of fuel economy. They concentrated on cooking for domestic consumption, to the exclusion of other stove uses and products. They were based upon a largely centralized approach to innovation, which permitted only limited involvement by potential users in the process of stove design. Heavy emphasis was placed upon rapid mass dissemination, which was to be achieved though a 'blueprint approach', where clear targets were set for the numbers of stoves to be adopted within particular periods of time. Finally, there was a widespread assumption that the magnitude of the social or external benefits to be gained justified the provision of substantial subsidies as an incentive to individual consumers.

These attitudes were to prove highly influential in shaping the initiative launched by the Sri Lankan Government in 1984, which forms the main subject of this chapter. Before turning to this directly, however, it will be helpful to look first at the technologies which the new programme sought to displace.

Determinants of stove designs and user practices in Sri Lanka

Patterns of food consumption and methods of preparation vary comparatively little from one part of Sri Lanka to another. Breakfast usually consists of wheat flour pancakes (*roti*), bread, or left-over rice with grated coconut and chillies (*sambol*). Rice is generally eaten twice a day, accompanied by two or more curries, made from vegetables or pulses. In addition, tea may be prepared from two to five times a day, with a kettle sometimes being left to simmer continuously, where people remain at home, and are not constrained by a shortage of fuel.

This general pattern is, however, subject to a degree of seasonal variation. The amount of rice consumed tends to fall before the harvest, and to increase after it, and large quantities of sweets are prepared in the period immediately preceding the New Year.

Consumption also differs by wealth, with richer households enjoying a wider range of dishes, and generally more nutritious foods. In urban areas there is a growing tendency for people to have packed lunches, which are either prepared early in the morning at home or purchased from street stalls. For all this, however, the range of situation encountered remains comparatively narrow, and is insufficient, in itself, to have created the need for major variations in stove design.

The way in which people cook determines the major parameters of stove design. The first requirement is that it should be possible to heat two dishes at the same time, one of which will generally be on a large fire, with the other simmering to its side. Second, there should be sufficient flexibility to provide intense heat for an average period of 30–40 minutes per dish, and a lower temperature at other points. Third, the fire should be easy to light and extinguish particularly under circumstances where a kettle is not kept simmering. Fourth, the amount of time required to tend the fire whilst cooking is taking place should be kept to a minimum, so as to enable the cook to engage simultaneously in other activities.

The stove is not, however, only used for cooking for home consumption. In addition, it has to perform a number of other more minor functions, and these also have some bearing upon the design preferred. These include: smoking firewood, seeds and spices; parboiling paddy; boiling down honey; providing space heating in the early morning and evening; lighting homes during the night-time; and preparing sweets for sale. The precise significance of these additional factors varies by location, and according to the circumstances of individual households.

Design preferences are also a function of kitchen layout and house type. Poorer dwellings typically have kitchens with roofs constructed of coconut leaves (*cadjan*), through which smoke can pass without difficulty. The better-off, on the other hand, will normally construct kitchens with tiled roofs, where a chimney must be installed, at a cost of some Rs1500, to allow smoke to escape.

Traditional technology
Most Sri Lankan households cook either on a *U-chulah* or open-hearth stove, which varies relatively little in design from one place to another. They have no chimney, and are built with one side left open for the insertion of fuel. Sometimes stoves stand at floor level, and sometimes they are constructed on a platform of up to a metre in height. A wooden frame, which can be used for drying fuel and other products, is generally installed above the stove.

Stoves are normally built by the users themselves and incur little or no financial cost. The work takes about two hours, and the stoves then have to be resurfaced at regular intervals using a slurry of mud and cow dung. If maintained well, they will generally last for about 10 years. Two units are usually placed side by side, with a shared central wall, so that separate dishes may be prepared at the same time.

This design is used by the great majority of households in the Hill Country,[6] as well as in the rubber-growing areas of the Wet Zone (see Table 6.1). It is also used by slightly less than half of all households in the Dry Zone and Wet Zone coconut areas, where fuel is more abundantly available, and the less energy-efficient three-stone stove is more popular. A small number of people use both types of stove together.

In the estates, nearly everybody relies on the mud stove, whilst in urban areas the situation is a little more complicated. Most households still follow the practices of their

Table 6.1: Cookers used by rural households (percentages)

Zone	Using mud stove exclusively	Using 3-stone exclusively	Combining mud stove and 3-stone	Other combinations
Hill Country	88.4	5.8		5.8
Wet Zone (rubber)	72.1	23.5	2.9	1.5
Wet Zone (coconut)	45.7	51.0	1.3	2.0
Dry Zone	39.4	58.8	0.9	0.9

Source: adapted from Wijesinghe (1983, p.277)

rural counterparts, but substantial minorities combine the use of biomass stoves with electrical, gas or kerosene-burning devices.

The new stove

The design phase

In the period from the early 1950s to the late 1970s, a series of attempts were made by private individuals, government and non-government organizations to introduce new stove designs, but in Sri Lanka, as elsewhere, none of these achieved any significant impact.[7] All this was to change in 1979, when Sarvodaya, the country's largest non-government organization, began to get involved.

Sarvodaya had been founded in 1958 to promote an integrated approach to rural development based upon the principle of widespread participation, and a reassertion of traditional cultural values of co-operation and self-reliance. It supported many different types of activity, the most important of which were pre-schools and health work in rural communities.

These general priorities were broadly reflected in the four major objectives of the stove programme, which were:

○ to assist rural women by reducing the amount of time which they had to spend gathering fuel and cooking;

○ to improve their health by lessening exposure to smoke during the cooking process;

○ to reduce the general level of dirt in the kitchen, thus creating a more pleasant and more hygienic working environment;

○ to protect the environment by reducing the need for people to cut down trees for firewood.

Whilst sharing the fuelwood conservation objective characteristic of most other initiatives dating from this period, it is important to note that the Sarvodaya approach also exhibited features which were not to gain general currency in stoves circles until considerably later.

Support for their efforts came from a number of quarters. An American volunteer, who subsequently joined the ITDG Intermediate Technology Development Group Stoves Programme, was responsible for setting up the early tests.

114

Financial help was provided by Novib (Holland), Helvetas (Switzerland) and Vita and ATI (USA). Other members of ITDG made technical inputs from time to time, and contacts with other Asian non-governmental organizations, most notably Dian Desa (Indonesia) and Gandhiniketan Ashram (India), also proved influential.

The process of designing a stove was to take three years, with four different broad possibilities being explored and rejected before a satisfactory solution was arrived at.[8]

Initially, attempts were made to popularize the Lorena stove, which was used extensively by peasants in Guatemala. The model had four pot holes, a chimney, and a special combustion chamber which was claimed to lead to substantial fuel savings. This represented a radical departure from existing practice, and it quickly became apparent that it would not appeal to Sri Lankan users.

It was far larger than the *U-chulah*, took much longer to make, and could only be constructed by specialist stove builders, all of which made it much more expensive. The incorporation of a chimney made it more difficult to light, and added to total cooking time. Two of the four holes were redundant, and total fuel consumption actually increased.

This initial failure prompted Sarvodaya to look more closely at existing designs and practices, and out of this process arose the idea of a modified mud stove. Whilst retaining a chimney, this was smaller and easier to construct than the Lorena, and tests showed that it could improve upon the performance of the *U-chulah* in terms both of cooking time and of fuel conservation. However, certain difficulties still remained.

The mixtures from which the stoves were made were found to be unsatisfactory, leading to crumbling and deterioration in performance after only a short period of use. The design also demanded a relatively high level of skill on the part of the builder, and many failures were reported.

The next stove to be tested was the *tungku lowon*, an Indonesian design which was brought to Sarvodaya's attention by representatives of Dian Desa. This differed from its predecessor in a number of respects. The walls were made thinner, thus enlarging the combustion chamber and tunnel, air holes were incorporated, and the second hole was placed at a higher level than the first. The combined effect of these modifications was further savings in cooking time and fuel consumption. In addition, an

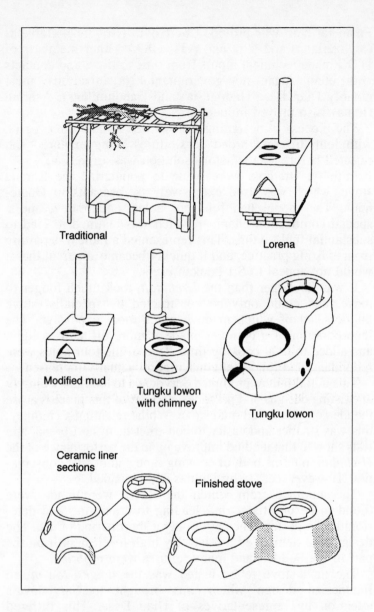

Figure 6.1: *Six generations of stove design*

improved mixture was developed, which lessened the problem of crumbling, and a new building technique, involving the use of moulds, was devised which reduced construction time and cost.

This represented a significant advance, but the retention of a chimney meant that costs could still not be reduced to a level where mass dissemination would become feasible. Since, by this stage, it was becoming apparent to the design team that rural households accorded only relatively low priority to a reduction in smoke levels, the logical next step was simply to do away with the chimney altogether.

Two other modifications were made at the same time. Smoke vents were incorporated around the second hole and the fire-hole was repositioned slightly, so as to make it easier to insert fuel whilst cooking. This reduced construction time and cost, and led to a simpler design, which could be built and disseminated more rapidly. At the same time, the elimination of the chimney reduced lighting-up time, thus giving the new stove a perceptible overall advantage in time saved over existing practices, which earlier versions had lacked.

For all these improvements, however, the new design was still not quite ready for mass dissemination. Although the level of skill demanded of builders had been significantly reduced, construction still depended upon the participation of trained Sarvodaya personnel, and still could not be completed within the space of a single day. This placed a rather severe limit upon the number of stoves which any individual could build, as well as leading to a situation where most stoves were being installed in the homes of the wealthier village households with whom workers tended to have closer contacts.

Second, whilst design tolerance had been increased, in the sense that a greater variation in basic dimensions could be entertained without having any adverse effect upon performance, a significant number of stoves was still found, on inspection, not to be reaching the required standard.

By mid-1982, some three years after the search for a new design began, a solution to this final set of problems was identified. This was based on the experience of an Indian programme. It involved potters being trained to produce standardized two-piece ceramic liners, which could be assembled in users' homes, and coated by a slurry of mud and cow dung to produce a stove which, in its final appearance, corresponded closely to the chimneyless *tungku lowon*.

With individual potters able to produce between 150 and 200 liners a month, and with installation simplified, so that stoves meeting uniform specifications could be constructed by semi-skilled builders in about four hours, the final major bottleneck was broken. The fact that adopters would have to pay Rs25 for their liners, where traditional designs could be installed at little or no financial cost, remained a potential constraint, but given that a reliable design had now been arrived at which provided the same facilities as traditional technology, whilst apparently offering significant advances in time saving and fuel economy, Sarvodaya felt confident that it could be promoted on an extensive basis.

This confidence was subsequently justified by a programme mounted in Kandy District, which is still continuing, and which has been responsible for the installation of several thousand of the new stoves.

Mass dissemination under the NFCP
The impetus for further expansion was provided in 1984, when the Ministry of Power and Energy (MPE) launched the National Fuelwood Conservation Programme (NFCP).

The rationale for the NFCP was outlined in a document prepared by Munasinghe.[9] This included a number of statements which implicitly questioned the orthodox approach to stove promotion which obtained at the time,[10] but any doubts which the author may have hinted at on this score appear ultimately to have been set aside.

The end result was a conventional formulation, where fuel saving was seen as the only real objective, and where there was to be an exclusive focus on cooking for domestic consumption. No other stoves apart from the one designed by Sarvodaya were to be promoted. Ambitious targets for dissemination were set, the most modest of which entailed coverage of approximately half of the nation's households by 1989. Heavy subsidies were to be provided on the grounds that deforestation on a catastrophic scale would occur if rapid and large-scale adoption did not take place, and that the balance of payments would be adversely affected as people switched to imported kerosene in the longer term.

The central assumptions of the programme are neatly encapsulated in a government poster from the period. In the top right-hand corner, a fierce sun beats down on a landscape which has been denuded of trees to provide fuel for the pot boiling away on a three-stone fire. In the centre there is a large picture of the new stove. Beneath it, a set of progressively larger trees depict the process of reforestation which will arise as it is adopted.

Aid donors were quick to offer their support for the initiative. The Dutch and the Norwegians led the way, by providing funding for work within the Integrated Rural Development Programme (IRDP) in Ratnapura and Hambantota in 1985. At the same time, the MPE itself embarked upon a joint programme to promote more extensive adoption in Kandy, with the Ministry of Local Government, Housing and Construction. By the end of the year a number of training programmes for potters and stove builders had been organized, and several thousand stoves had been installed in the three districts.

The following year, a much larger initiative, covering the districts of Kurunegala, Kegalle, Gampaha, Kalutara, Matale, Kandy and Nuwara Eliya, was started under the Sri Lanka-Netherlands Energy Programme.[11] The picture was then completed with the addition of further IRDPs in Matara in 1987 and in Moneragala in 1988, which were funded by SIDA and NORAD (the Swedish and Norwegian government aid agencies) respectively.

Each district had a co-ordinating officer (DCO) appointed by the programme who, together with staff under his supervision, was made responsible for training potters and stove builders, and for the procurement and distribution of liners. The precise manner in which this would be done would, however, differ according to local circumstances. Sometimes the DCO would work through the local AGA office which, in turn, would either arrange for stoves to be promoted through their own extension network, or through voluntary organizations operating at the village level. Sometimes, the DCO would bypass the AGA altogether, either making his own arrangements with voluntary bodies, or organizing mass dissemination exercises through direct contact with adopters. Finally, in certain instances, stove builders themselves would act as their own extension agents.

There were also variations in the costs of production and distribution, as well as in the ways in which costs were allocated between users and external agencies. Initially, in Kandy, potters and stove builders were each paid Rs15, all of which was then recovered from users. This left Sarvodaya responsible only for the direct costs of extension, transport and administration, which together generally amounted to a

119

further Rs10 a stove. Of a total cost of Rs40, before account was taken of training and overheads, three-quarters was therefore carried by the user.

The MPE began with a similar system, but when the IRDPs started to get involved, a new, and more heavily subsidized alternative was introduced, which only required the user to pay the Rs15 builder's fee.

Although failing to meet the ambitious targets set initially, records suggest that the programme had led to the installation of some 96000 stoves by the beginning of 1988 (see Table 6.2). The longer-term objective was revised downwards at that point to install 500000 stoves in rural areas by 1993, and a further 100000 in urban areas by 1990.

Substantial gains are claimed to have followed. These incorporate the initial, primarily social objectives anticipated by Munasinghe, subsequently extended to include community and private benefits, which were given less prominence in the initial phases. A comprehensive list is spelt out in an article appearing in *Boiling Point*.[12] This is summarized in Table 6.3, and provides a starting point for the assessment which follows in the next section.

Table 6.2: Number of domestic stoves installed under the initial programme[1]

District	1985	1986	1987	Total
Kurunegala		3 810	17 101	20 911
Ratnapura	4 883	7 783	8 077	20 743
Hambantota	9 118	6 170	?	15 288
Kandy	1 231	3 673	6 824	11 728
Kegalle		853	6 786	7 639
Matara			6 394	6 394
Gampaha		2 211	3 511	5 722
Nuwara Eliya		655	2 679	3 334
Matale			3 176	3 176
Kalutara		297	717	1 014
Total	15 232	25 452	55 265	95 949

Source: Amarasekera (1988).
1. Excludes the specifically urban stove programme

Table 6.3: Benefits claimed by the NFCP as a result of the adoption of the new stove

INDIVIDUAL BENEFITS
○ Less money is spent on firewood
○ Less time is used collecting, transporting and chopping wood
○ Cooking time is reduced
○ The time saved can be used elsewhere
○ Smoke is reduced, making the kitchen more hygienic, and reducing eye, skin and respiratory diseases
○ Exposure to the danger of open fires is reduced
○ The use of boiled water is encouraged

COMMUNITY BENEFITS
○ Job opportunities are created for stove builders
○ The traditional pottery industry is revived

NATIONAL BENEFITS
○ Deforestation and its harmful consequences are reduced
○ The need for investment and land to be devoted to fuelwood plantations is reduced
○ 70000 tonnes of firewood are served each year (which is enough to satisfy the requirements of 36000 additional households)
○ The rate of increase of fuelwood prices is reduced

An assessment of the NFCP

Research methods

These claims may now be investigated, using a combination of primary and secondary sources. The primary evidence derives mainly from surveys of adopters and non-adopters drawn from peri-urban and rural areas in Kandy and Hambantota. Kandy was chosen because it afforded the longest experience of stoves programmes, whilst Hambantota had the largest concentration of new stoves at the time the research was carried out. Some use will also be made of data gathered in other communities on the ways in which women distribute their time between different activities.

Secondary sources consist of surveys carried out by other people in Sri Lanka, and of more general materials on other stove programmes.

They are used especially in cases where claims were only published after fieldwork had been completed, and had not been fully anticipated at the time when the research was planned.

Many of the issues to be investigated pose quite complicated methodological problems. Nevertheless, the evidence available, whilst less than totally conclusive on all scores, is generally sufficient to arrive at a reasonable impression both of how rural people have responded to the programme, and of the underlying factors by which their behaviour has been guided.[13]

Community benefits
Of the benefits claimed for the project, those arising at the community level are the most straightforward, and will be dealt with first. Figures presented by Amarasekera[14] suggest that by 1988, employment had been created for 73 potter families and 314 stove builders, generating additional income of Rs1.24 and Rs0.92 million respectively. There is no reason to suppose that these do not present a reasonably accurate picture.

The private and social (or national) benefits which have been claimed for the NFCP present more serious analytical problems. In order to assess their validity, it will first of all be necessary to explore certain prior aspects of the adoption process.

Numbers of stoves disseminated
The first of these concerns the number of stoves disseminated, an indication of which is conveyed by Table 6.2.

The problem here is that it is difficult to determine the accuracy of these figures. In Kandy, where the process began, and where a build-up in numbers took place over a period of years, our impression was that official records corresponded closely to the situation on the ground. In Hambantota, where expansion took place far more rapidly in response to perceived national imperatives, larger discrepancies were noted. Several persons recorded as having adopted stoves could not be located, and others who had stoves did not appear on official lists.

The net effect of such factors could not be precisely accounted for in the time available, but it seems probable that the records investigated generally overstated the extent of actual adoption. If this experience were reproduced elsewhere, this would mean that official national totals should be regarded as ceiling figures, which do not necessarily reflect actual levels achieved.

A profile of adopters

The next step is to ask who has been able to take advantage of the new stove. Our enquiries, based on 300 interviews and comparing the economic status of adopters and non-adopters, provides clear evidence that users are concentrated to a disproportionate extent amongst the relatively better off. This relationship is especially clear in Kandy.

Studies of innovation have, however, often identified a tendency for the relatively wealthy to adopt early, with the poorer following at a later stage. In the light of this possibility, time series data were investigated for indications that the disparity might prove to be temporary in nature, but no evidence of this could be found. It should also be noted that the association between economic status and adoption was probably understated, because of the way in which non-adopters were selected for interview.[15]

In the light of the factors discussed, it therefore seems reasonable to conclude that inequalities in access to the new stove are both substantial and enduring in nature. There would seem to be three possible explanations for this.

It is fairly clear, from informal interviews carried out with officials and users, that the dissemination process itself was structured in such a way as to increase the likelihood of adoption by the relatively well off. The priority attached by the president to energy conservation translated into considerable pressure, at each descending level in the implementing hierarchy, for rapid dissemination, and this was reinforced by actual cash incentives for officials who were able to encourage people to adopt. Under these circumstances, officials at the local level, apart from adopting themselves, inevitably turned first to the professional and business communities who constituted their natural peer group. They also showed a strong tendency to focus their attention on the peri-urban areas and smaller rural towns, where concentrations of population assisted more rapid dissemination, and where disproportionate numbers of better-off households were to be found.

A number of enquiries, including our own, has suggested that many people hesitate to install a new stove until they are in a position to upgrade their kitchen into a more permanent structure. Since semi-permanent kitchens are found far more frequently in the homes of poorer people, this could well explain a part of the disparity which has been observed.

123

In principle it seems possible that some poorer households will be deterred by the cost of the stove, especially where fuel is only gathered, and reductions in consumption do not therefore translate into financial gains.[16] A discussion of fuel savings will help to throw more light on this point.

A profile of fuel sources

We now move on to the question of where people obtained their fuel, which was also covered in the 300-household survey referred to earlier – confining ourselves, for simplicity's sake, to the single major individual source drawn upon by each household.

The first significant feature to note is the importance of purchased fuel, which is particularly marked in the peri-urban areas. This category encompasses a number of different biomass fuels. In the eastern part of Hambantota, it would generally comprise wood brought in by cart from *chenas* after they had been cleared for cultivation. In the west, it would be more likely to have been residues from sawmills or cinnamon sticks. In Kandy, both rubber wood from Kalutara, and jungle wood from the Mahaweli clearances to the north of the Hill Country would be used.

Home gardens were also an important source. These were utilized to a significant extent in all of the locations covered, and were particularly important in rural communities, as we have already seen in Chapter 3. Coconut by-products were by far the most common individual fuel here, although in the drier areas of Hambantota these gave way to various drought-resistant shrubs.

We also found that a substantial number of people who had no gardens of their own, or who had insufficient land to satisfy their requirements, were able to gather fuel from other people's land. Once again, this pattern arose more frequently in the rural than in the peri-urban areas.

Other sources were of little overall importance, but could be of some significance in particular locations. Government land, cleared and cultivated illegally by encroachers, yielded a considerable amount of fuel as a by-product for rural people in Hambantota, whilst forested areas on tea estate land could be of considerable local significance in rural Kandy.

Superimposed upon these differences between rural and peri-urban, and Hill Country and Dry Zone areas are equally clear distinctions between households of different economic status. Rich households relied almost exclusively upon either purchased or home garden fuel. Those in the middle of the spectrum depended much more heavily on home gardens than anything else. The poor were generally obliged to purchase if they lived in peri-urban locations, or to travel substantial distances to collect their requirements in the case of rural communities.

Fuel savings

The next aspect to be considered is fuel savings, although, for a number of reasons, these are difficult to assess.

To start with, several factors make it hard to establish a satisfactory baseline. Within an overall framework of broadly similar practices, the specific way in which cooking is performed may vary, in certain respects, from one person, and from one period of time, to another. Behaviour also tends to be adapted where fuel becomes more difficult to find.[17] A wide range of results may thus be obtained, even where the same basic design of stove is being used.

There are similar problems in assessing the performance of the new stove under field conditions, with results obtained in laboratories representing only the maximum potential saving, and providing no clear indication of the actual norm.[18] Account also needs to be taken of variations in performance between newly installed and older models.[19]

In the light of these difficulties, and of the limited resources available for data collection, no attempt was made physically to measure fuel consumption. We relied instead upon informants' reported impressions of relative levels of pre- and post-adoption use.

This procedure was not entirely satisfactory. It is unlikely that those who did not purchase fuel had a very accurate sense of the quantities used. Account must also be taken of the possibility that people may sometimes have been inclined to exaggerate savings in line with their perception of what interviewers wanted to hear.

As such, the figures obtained, which suggested savings in the range of 25–50 per cent in Kandy, and of a little less than 25 per cent in Hambantota, must be interpreted with caution. This is especially so in view of the results of another survey, which indicated that 26 per cent of adopters continued to use their old stoves for at least a part of the time.[20] Our findings are, however, roughly in line with those of other surveys and, taking this into account, the claim by the Energy Unit of average savings of 20 per cent is probably not unreasonable.

Private financial benefits

We may now turn from the various sets of background data to a more direct assessment of the private and social benefits which the NFCP is said to have brought about.

The new stove potentially offers two types of financial benefits for the households which adopt them: there are the direct savings achieved in the case of those who purchase fuel; and there is the indirect contribution to household income, arising if time saved in fuel collection and cooking can then be redeployed in some form of income-generating activity. Only the first of these possibilities will be considered here, with discussion of the second being deferred to the wider review, which follows, of time effects.

Drawing together data on average fuel expenditures and likely fuel savings, it seems that households which purchase all of their requirements would be approximately Rs1 a day better off after adopting the new stove. Although apparently small, this figure may be significant. It promises a pay-back period of only 15 days, and even where the full unsubsidized price is taken into account, the stove would still have paid for itself within two months.

Savings may also be measured in relation to household income, and would account for perhaps 3 per cent of the amount on which a poor household, dependent upon wage labour, would have to support itself. To put this figure in its proper perspective, however, it should be recalled that the poor were less likely to purchase fuel than the well off (especially in rural areas), and that they were also considerably less likely to have adopted new stoves than their wealthier counterparts. It would therefore probably be reasonable to conclude that the financial savings achieved would have been of no more than marginal significance to most adopters.

Time savings

Questions of time savings raise similar methodological problems and, once again, we were obliged to rely exclusively upon what informants told us. Similar caveats about data reliability therefore apply.

126

In principle, two general types of savings could arise with a new stove: all users could potentially benefit from reductions in cooking time; and for those not wholly dependent upon purchased fuel, there was also the possibility of achieving reductions in the time devoted to gathering and processing.

As far as cooking time was concerned, there was a very widespread perception that the new stove was of benefit. Users reported an average saving in the region of a third, which is equivalent to a little less than an hour each day for the average household. In response to a separate question, they also indicated that saving in cooking time was, in their estimation, the most important individual gain arising from stove use although, in some communities, fuel savings were regarded as of equal significance.

The value of this time is difficult to calculate, since it arises in small bits and pieces on a regular basis each day. No direct enquiries were conducted into the subject, but given the limited opportunities which existed for income-generating activities around the home, it seems unlikely that many women would have been able to have translated this into a direct financial gain. The most likely outcome would thus appear to have been an increase in the care and attention devoted to other aspects of unpaid household work, although enhanced leisure time might also have been a possibility in some cases.

People found it more difficult to estimate changes in fuel collection and processing times, but the general consensus was that these were less significant. Where home gardens provided the major source, collection would tend to take place on a daily basis and the pattern and the implications of any savings arising would have been similar to those discussed in relation to cooking time. Where fuel was gathered from further afield, one of two situations might have arisen: either the work was done regularly throughout the year, or it was concentrated into limited seasonal windows of opportunity, as in the case of clippings from tea estates. In such instances, admittedly rare, the time would have had a clear opportunity cost in the form of wage-labouring employment foregone. But taking time as a whole, it must be concluded that although significant savings are achieved, these seem unlikely, under most circumstances, to have led to enhanced opportunities for income generation.

Health benefits

Nearly all of the discussion here must be based on secondary sources, and none will be conclusive.

A number of possible connections have been posited in the international literature, between the adoption of more fuel-efficient stoves and the health of those who cook, or spend time in the kitchen.[21] The most important, but also the most complex, of these concerns the potential benefits of reduced exposure to smoke. This, in turn, breaks down into two smaller questions.

The first is whether a more efficient stove will necessarily lead to reduced exposure to smoke. In so far as there is a reduction in overall cooking time, and in the time within this period when the cook must attend the fire, then the answer must be yes. The contribution must also be positive in so far as fuel savings, at the margin, help to avoid substitution from preferred into inferior, smokier fuels.[22]

Where the type of fuel used remains the same, the question of whether the level of smoke emitted, during the time when the stove is operating, is itself reduced, is more difficult to determine.

The literature suggests that improved fuel economy is normally achieved by way of increased combustion efficiency, and that this, in turn, generally goes hand in hand with a reduction in potentially harmful emissions. Improved heat transmission is sometimes achieved at the expense of combustion efficiency, however, and can therefore have the opposite effect. From this point of view, even if the new stoves do require less fuel, it is therefore only likely, and not certain, that exposure to smoke will be reduced.

The second issue is whether exposure to smoke leads to disease. Partly as a result of the low priority accorded to it by medical researchers, and partly because of the difficulty of linking causes and effects separated from each other by long periods of time, firm causal connections have yet to be established. Potentially dangerous levels of nitrogen dioxide, carbon monoxide and a range of individual carbon-containing chemicals have, however, been recorded in environments where biomass-burning stoves are in use, and there are strong grounds for supposing that smoke is implicated in a number of different health problems. These are thought to include: acute respiratory infections; chronic obstructive lung diseases, such as bronchitis; low birthweight, together with all of the subsequent problems with which this is associated; and certain cancers and eye problems. Of these, the respiratory infections are probably the most serious, since these are now recognized as one of the two principal causes of childhood illness and death in the Third World.

On this point, it would thus seem reasonable to conclude that more efficient stoves will probably have beneficial long-term health effects, both for the women who use them and for the children who spend time with them in the kitchen. But a final point to be borne in mind here is that even if the benefits are real, they are much less readily perceptible to the beneficiaries than other changes attendant upon stove use, and may therefore have little or no effect on adoption behaviour. It should also be remembered that a certain amount of smoke is valued for drying, making it desirable, from the user's own point of view, that it should only be reduced to a point where this secondary function is not impaired.

The second health advantage claimed for stoves is that the availability of an additional pot hole will encourage people to boil their drinking water, thus reducing the incidence of diarrhoeal diseases. There is clearly the potential for behaviour to be modified in this way, and this is pointed out to prospective adopters. Our own investigations, however, revealed that few users were actually taking advantage of this possibility.

Another claim is that the new stove contributes to improved safety in the kitchen in a number of ways. The fact that the fire is more enclosed is thought to reduce the danger of fuel falling out, or of loose garments catching fire. It is also argued that the pots fit better, and are thus more stable and unlikely to be accidentally tipped over. These claims are plausible, but no hard evidence is available to confirm their veracity, or indicate the precise significance of the contribution made.

Much the same applies to the suggestion that exposure of food and utensils to dirt, stray animals and vermin[23] is reduced where people are encouraged to construct a platform, upon which the stove stands, when the stove itself is built. Finally, it has also been claimed that lowering fuel consumption leads to a reduction in the work of carrying fuel, and in the back problems with which this is believed to be associated.

Other private benefits

Taking the evidence on private benefits as a whole, it would seem fair to conclude that this generally supports the claims made on behalf of the new stoves whilst, at the same time, suggesting that some of the advantages may not be very large. Financial savings, where they arise at all, are not normally of great significance. Time savings are more widely valued, but difficult to quantify, and probably only of marginal significance for the majority of users. Health benefits, on the other hand, whilst potentially of far greater value, may not be perceived at all by most adopters.

Considered together, these factors therefore do not add up to a very convincing case from the potential user's point of view, and would not, by themselves, seem to provide a sufficient explanation of why such large numbers of stoves have been adopted. Whilst hard evidence is once again lacking, it might, therefore, be useful to speculate about other forces which may have been at work.

From this point of view, it seems very likely that the enthusiasm with which the stove was promoted was a major factor. Support from the highest level of government provided a powerful impetus, and this was reinforced by targets and individual incentives for those dealing directly with adopters. The major evidence for such an effect is found in the fact that a high proportion of adopters is drawn from relatively well-off households, who would appear to have comparatively little to gain from adoption, but who, by virtue of living around the urban centres in which those promoting the stove were based, were most likely to be approached. In addition, there is a certain amount of evidence to suggest that the new stove has become something of a status symbol, often being adopted for this reason, rather than for any perceived value which it might possess.

Finally, it seems probable that some adopters were heavily influenced by the size of the subsidy offered, although most claim that they would be prepared to pay the full price when a replacement is required.

The impact on the rate of deforestation

Given that stoves were not being targeted towards poorer households, the case for subsidies could not be made on welfare grounds. It must, therefore, stand or fall on the strength of the social advantages of adoption. These may now be investigated, starting with the claimed contribution to a reduction in the level of deforestation.

To establish the extent to which deforestation may have been averted, one has to take the average level of savings arising (assumed to be 20 per cent), and multiply that by the amount of fuel which is both extracted from forest land, and is in excess of the sustainable yield or increment which that land could provide.

The proportion of fuel taken from forests cannot be determined with precision from the survey discussed on page 124, as this only provides information on the major individual source each household is using. It describes neither the subsidiary sources of those mainly dependent on the forests, nor the subsidiary use of forests by others, but additional data collected make it clear that these limitations make little difference.

On the basis of the data presented, a number of points are fairly clear:

○ The fuel obtained from the users' own home gardens, or from the gardens of others, accounts for approximately half of all consumption in three of the four types of community investigated, and makes no contribution to deforestation at all.

○ The government land, which supplies 38 per cent of rural, and 7 per cent of peri-urban consumption in Hambantota, is all *chena*. In other words, it has already been cleared for slash-and-burn cultivation, and the fuel obtained is a by-product of this process. So even if the land previously had trees growing on it, the fact that fuel is now being extracted from it is an effect, and not a cause, of their being removed.

○ The land classified as 'other', which provides a small proportion of the fuel used in Hambantota, is upland of a similar type, and is used either for *chena* or for more permanent cultivation. The only difference is that it is not encroached upon, but is operated under different types of government licence. As such, no fuel extracted here can be contributing to deforestation either.

In the overall category of gathered fuels, this then leaves only the estate and other forests, which are used by relatively small numbers of households in rural Kandy. Together they only account for just over 4 per cent of the total samples and, even here, it is unlikely that all fuel obtained from this source is causing a problem.

Regulations dictate that only dead wood should be gathered, and it is in any case more convenient for people themselves to collect fuel of this kind whenever it is available. Whilst some cutting almost certainly does occur, this is therefore unlikely to be extensive, and, even then, it would still have to be demonstrated that the amount cut exceeded the annual growth increment, and that whole trees rather than branches were being cut down.

Finally, there is the question of whether purchased fuel might be causing deforestation. Our enquiries revealed that, in Hambantota, all fuel was coming from *chena* land and, so, could not be a contributory factor. In Kandy, two sources were utilized: rubber wood from estate clearances, which could immediately be ruled out, and former forest land, which had been cleared in the Dry Zone to the north of the Hill Country under the Mahaweli scheme. This means that, once again here, fuel production is only a consequence, and not an agent of deforestation.

Putting all of this evidence together, one arrives at the conclusion that new stoves are currently helping to reduce deforestation to the tune of approximately 20 per cent of 4 per cent of present fuel consumption by stove adopters. The final figure, in other words must be less than one per cent of their total consumption. This is a modest figure by any standard, and makes a nonsense of calculations based upon the assumption that all current fuel saving will translate directly into forests saved. It also suggests that any effect of stoves on fuel prices is likely to be marginal, even in the areas where they are most heavily concentrated.

Foreign exchange savings
Even if fuelwood extraction were not contributing to deforestation, it is still possible that shortages would cause people to substitute imported kerosene, thus justifying a stove subsidy on the grounds that it could save foreign exchange. Evidence from other countries, where fuel shortages are already more of a problem, indicates, however, that this is unlikely to happen. This suggests that people substitute into more valuable fuels only when their incomes grow, but not as the prices of their present fuels increase.

Where price increases are encountered, two reactions are normal: consumption is cut back by more careful use of the fuels already available; and subsequently, if prices continue on an upward trend, substitution into inferior fuels, such as crop residues, tends to take place.

There is limited evidence that the first change is already occurring in Sri Lanka. We also found some cases of the second type of change taking place in fieldwork locations in Kandy and Hambantota.

The new urban stove programme

Background
Shortly before we finished collecting data on the rural stoves programme in the second half of 1987, a new initiative was launched. This was based upon a modified version of the Sarvodaya stove, but was aimed at the urban market, and involved much more extensive participation by the private sector. The idea was still in its infancy and although it clearly had the potential to address some of the key limitations which have been identified in relation to its predecessor, it was too early to arrive at any assessment of its performance at that stage. However, documents supplied by ITDG since that time have made it possible to arrive at some broad conclusions about the course of events[24] and these are recorded below.

The new approach in outline
The new stove arises from collaboration between the Ceylon Electricity Board (CEB), ITDG and a small number of private-sector tile manufacturers from Negombo, which lies a short distance to the north of Colombo.

Two basic designs have been promoted. The more important is the Anagi 2. This is identical to the Sarvodaya model, except that it is made in one piece, and can therefore be used without first having to be covered with a mud and cow-dung slurry. This has two important effects: the stove can now be bought and utilized 'off the shelf', whereas its forerunner could only be installed with the assistance of a semi-skilled specialist; and it becomes portable, which is an important consideration in urban environments where people are much more likely to move, and where space is often at a premium.[25] The other new design is the Anagi 1, a one-pot

133

version of the same stove which has only played a relatively minor part in the new promotion, and which will therefore largely be disregarded in what follows.[26]

The CEB and ITDG decided to involve private manufacturers from the outset. They also decided to eliminate all direct subsidies on the new stove in order to create a system which would not depend upon government support for its long-term survival (although no alternative could be found in the early stages to heavy official involvement in marketing). The initial intention was to sell 100000 stoves annually on the Colombo market at a price in the region of Rs40. With stoves requiring replacement, on average, once every two years, this would then have created sufficient demand for manufacturers to enjoy adequate returns on their investments.

It was envisaged that subsequent phases might first entail the extension of activities to other major urban centres. Ultimately, there would then be a move into the rural areas, where the new design would be produced by retrained potters, and where it would progressively displace the Sarvodaya stove over a period of about five years.

It was recognized that adopters would, in the first instance, most probably be drawn predominantly from the ranks of the relatively well off. This could be justified as a means of creating the mass demand which manufacturers would require to reduce their costs and bring prices down to a level where poorer households could more readily afford to adopt for themselves. At the same time, it was recognized that some form of targeted subsidies would most likely be required if the full spectrum of fuel users were to benefit. Rather than creating new systems, it was hoped that existing channels for the provision of subsidized credit could be utilized for this purpose.

Assessment
The targets for the Colombo market were to prove over-ambitious. Cost-cutting mass production techniques proved difficult to implement, and this was reflected in a higher than anticipated retail price of Rs65. At the same time, demand was somewhat lower than expected, and is now running at between 60 and 70000 stoves a year.

These figures should, however, be put in their proper perspective. In relation to the NFCP, which itself compares very favourably with what has generally been the case else-where, they represent a rapid rate of adoption, and this provides a more relevant yardstick than any notional abso-lute targets can provide.

Initial adoption rates only tell a part of the story, however, and it is necessary to probe a little further before ariving at any final conclusions. The evidence, at this point, becomes a little thin, although still pointing firmly towards a positive assessment. The major findings arising to date are as follows.

A small survey indicated that nearly two-thirds of adopters were continuing to use their stoves 21 months after purchase, which appears a rather good figure in the light of an antici-pated average lifetime of two years, although little is pre-sently known about readoption rates.

Some evidence of cracking and other forms of deteriora-tion have come to light, but these do not seem to have had a significant adverse effect upon performance.

Field tests indicate fuel savings of the order of 25 per cent, which compare favourably with the results of comparable tests on the Sarvodaya model.

Finally, the impact of the savings achieved is also greater, in so far as urban consumers are far more likely to purchase fuel than their rural counterparts. According to one calcula-tion, a household buying half of its fuel could expect to save about Rs26 a month.

On the basis of these figures, the project as a whole is believed to offer a very attractive rate of return. In addition to benefits accruing to consumers, it has also served to create a significant amount of employment, and has probably led to the preservation of jobs in the pottery industry which might otherwise have been lost.

As anticipated, the initial experience of the new stove suggested that only a very small number of low-income households were willing or able to adopt. It is believed that cost is the key to non-adoption, although no conclusive proof to this effect has been presented. In mitigation of this failure to reach the poorer households, it might be argued that the project could still be in the early adoption phase, where a disproportionate number of high-income purchasers is to be anticipated. In addition, the econo-mies-of-scale arguments advanced above remain valid. It could also be argued that anything which reduces demand will ease upward pressure on prices for all consumers, irrespective of whether they have adopted or not.

It was never supposed that the new stove would contribute to a significant reduction in the rate of deforestation, and calculations made some two years into the implementation phase reaffirm that this is the case. At the same time, and despite the lack of any expression of ambition in this direction, it is probable that the new stove does rather better against this criterion than its Sarvodaya counterpart.

Conclusion

The evidence reviewed suggests that the stoves promoted under the NFCP have certainly had some positive effect on the lives of the people who have adopted them, but have fallen a long way short of achieving the rather grandiose objectives by which the programme was guided. Viewed in these terms, the initiative could be regarded as no more than a limited success.

The most important contrasts between the Sarvodaya stove, as it was promoted through the NFCP, and the more recent semi-privatized Anagi 2 system, are summarized in Table 6.4.

Table 6.4: Two programmes at a glance

	Sarvodaya stove	Anagi 2 stove
First promoted	1982	1987
Retail price	Rs40 (1987)	Rs65 (1989)
Direct subsidy	62.5 per cent	Zero
Where promoted	Kandy, Gampaha, Nuwara Eliya, Matale, Matara, Hambantota, Ratnapura, Kegalle, Kurunegala	Initially: Colombo Subsequently: Kandy Gampaha, Nuwara Eliya, Badulla
Numbers adopted by 1990	232 000	81 000
Proposed adoptions in next phase	130 000	315 000
Average lifetime	3 years	2 years
Average fuel saving	20 per cent	25 per cent

Among other things, this shows that the Anagi is targeted on the areas of greatest fuel shortage, and as such represents a much more cost-effective route both to fuel savings, and to the other advantages which follow from this. It also cuts through much of the cumbersome apparatus previously required for dissemination, opening up the prospect of adoption on a much wider scale (although this conclusion would not necessarily extend to all *rural* areas, as we shall see in the final chapter). Finally, it appears, at least, to be no worse than the previous approach at reaching poorer households, and holds out the possibility that increasing numbers from within this category will be able to benefit as time goes by.

The overall conclusion to be drawn from these comparisons is therefore clear. The new approach represents a major advance over its predecessor and compares very favourably with what has been achieved in other countries.

Notes

1. Foley and Moss (1985).
2. Krugmann, (1987).
3. Joseph (1983).
4. Manibog (1984).
5. Foundation for Woodfuel Dissemination (1987).
6. The only exceptions are the higher areas where the combined effect of fuel scarcity and the need for space heating have encouraged a range of innovations. Ten different designs have been obvserved in the village of Hatton, for example, many of which imitate models first introduced into the area by Tamil estate workers from Southern India.
7. Amarasekera (1986).
8. For a more detailed account of the evolution of the new stove see Howes *et al.* (1983).
9. Munasinghe (1986).
10. At various points, Munasinghe appears to accept that fuelwood extraction is not a major cause of deforestation, that stoves should only be disseminated after it has been clearly established that there is a demand for them, and that no 'simple and universal' solutions are available.
11. The promotion of domestic stoves was only one element in a programme of activities which also covered innovations for use in the tea industry, solar energy, producer gas, industrial energy conservation and a number of smaller research activities. See Van der Knyff (1988).
12. Liyanage (1986).
13. For a more detailed statement of research methods, see Appendix.
14. Amarasekera and Sepalage (1988), p.24.
15. Interviewers were instructed to identify non-adopters by taking the

nearest households falling within this category to each adopter household covered. Since adopters were drawn to a disproportionate extent from the wealthier strata, there was naturally a tendency for this also to be true of their neighbours. If there had been time to select adopter and non-adopter households randomly from amongst all the households in (say) a district, this would have overcome the distorting effect of the tendency for new stoves, and hence our informants, to be concentrated in generally more prosperous areas.

16. Foley and Barnard (1984) have advanced this argument.
17. Krugmann (1987) suggests that efficiency of up to 20 per cent can even be achieved, under certain circumstances, with the three-stone stove. Foley and Barnard (1984) make a similar case.
18. Krugmann (1987).
19. Foley and Barnard (1984).
20. Sumanasekera (1986).
21. Smith (1987).
22. A small number of instances of this kind were encountered in the course of investigations in Hambantota.
23. Sumanasekera (1986) suggests that 88 per cent of households in Hambantota constructed platforms for their new stoves.
24. See Jones (1989) and Clarke (1990).
25. The stove can still be covered in a slurry if users wish. This has the advantage of improving strength and durability, but for the reasons indicated, only a fairly small minority of users take this measure.
26. The international record is poor. Comparatively few initiatives have advanced beyond the experimental stage. Even where this initial hurdle is overcome, Manibog (1984) finds a somewhat patchy record, with 20–30 per cent of the stoves installed only being used intermittently, and a further 10–20 per cent, not at all.

SECTION IV
CONCLUSION

7. Towards a new biomass strategy

The concluding chapter is divided into three parts. The first establishes an overall framework within which to take stock of the achievements and shortcomings of the farmers' woodlots and the NFCP. The second reviews common factors in the background of the two initiatives, which help to explain the difficulties which have been encountered, and then goes on to identify the differences which explain the greater degree of success attained in relation to stoves. The third is an attempt to establish a different set of principles upon which to base the relationship between government and rural people, which are then used to outline a new biomass strategy for Sri Lanka.

Performance in comparative perspective

Casley and Lury have developed a simple set of analytical tools for assessing project performance.[1] These distinguish between:

○ the various inputs which are supplied;
○ the immediate outputs to which these are meant to give rise;
○ the effects, both intended and unintended, which follow;
○ the longer-term impacts to which these eventually lead.

Using this framework, Figure 7.1 summarizes what the interventions were initially intended to achieve, and provides a baseline against which outcomes can then be compared.

In the case of the CFP, only the farmers' woodlot component is considered. For stoves, the statement of objectives is based on Munasinghe.[2]

Outputs

When actual performance is compared with intentions at the end of 1987, stoves are found to have reached 12.5 per cent of the installation target laid down in the document prepared by Munasinghe, whilst with woodlots only 4.4 per cent of the intended area had actually been planted.

Viewed in these absolute terms, both activities appear to have fallen a very long way short of their stated goals although, in relative terms, stoves seem to have done significantly better.

This, however, gives a misleadingly negative picture. Taking the woodlots first, earlier discussion indicated that external factors combined to depress the area planted to a much lower level than would otherwise have been possible, and whilst their effect cannot be quantified very precisely,

Table 7.1: The objectives of the interventions compared

	Farmers' woodlots	Stoves
Outputs	To establish 4055ha of woodlots by 1987	To install 2.64 million stoves by 1990
Effects	To increase fuelwood supply by 25000 cu.metres per year To raise general awareness of the need for, and means of increasing, fuel production	To reduce fuelwood consumption by 3.168 million tonnes per year
Private impacts	To raise the income of participating households by US$25–56 a year, according to plot size	To reduce annual fuel expenditure of rural, estate and urban households by US$2, US$8 and US$10 respectively[2]
Social impacts	To reduce deforestation and adverse effects upon the environment by an unspecified amount To make theoretical commercial energy savings of US$0.88 million per year[1]	To reduce deforestation and adverse effects upon the environment by an unspecified amount To make commercial energy savings of US$109 million per year[2]

1. 1981 prices
2. 1985 prices

142

their absence would certainly have elevated performance to at least 20 per cent of the original target. Even when this is taken into account, however, it remains clear that there was something fundamentally wrong with the package itself.

In the case of stoves, a rather different situation arises. Although much of the earlier discussion had reflected the formal position that all activities were taking place within the common framework of the NFCP, the reality was somewhat different. In practice, it was the individual IRDPs which provided the bulk of the required resources, which were making most of the decisions about implementation. If it had proved possible to assemble all targets set by individual districts, and to have compared those with actual stoves installed, some overall shortfall would still have been apparent, but it is almost certain that performance would have appeared in a much more favourable light.

Stoves therefore appear to have come much closer to achieving their intended level of outputs than woodlots. Furthermore, where stove targets were not met, shortfalls would have been accompanied by a nearly proportional reduction in the total cost of the intervention. Given the much higher start-up costs of the CFP, on the other hand, overall costs would only fall marginally for each hectare which remained unplanted. The effective cost per area of land planted, therefore, rises sharply as the size of the shortfall grows.

Effects and impacts
The extent to which intended outputs are achieved immediately imposes a ceiling upon the satisfaction of all other criteria.

Thus, although with woodlots it will be some time before it will be possible to measure precisely how much woodfuel production has increased, the low level of successful planting already means that only small increases in fuel supply will be possible. This can be stated without even starting to explore how much wood might actually end up as fuel, rather than being diverted to other possible end uses which growers generally favour. It also follows that the intended private impact of increasing participants' incomes could not be achieved to any significant extent. With stoves, the situation is more clear cut. Most available evidence points to the conclusion that substantial reductions in fuel consumption have been made.

As far as social impacts are concerned, each of the four preceding chapters provides strong evidence that, under present Sri Lankan conditions, neither reduced fuel consumption, nor expanded supply, is likely to have more than the tiniest effect upon the rate of deforestation, neither will they significantly affect the amount of energy which Sri Lanka must import.

Taking impacts as a whole, it may therefore be concluded that forestry fails by both private and social criteria, where stoves at least achieve a measure of private success. When the analysis is extended to take account of financial viability and longer-term sustainability, this conclusion is strengthened. It is inconceivable that woodlots could continue to spread if external support were to be withdrawn. Stoves, by contrast, might well survive this transition, as the early experience of the urban programme, discussed in Chapter 6, suggests.

The failure of both interventions to secure certain of their objectives may be explained by reference to common underlying features in the approaches pursued. The fact that stoves achieved a measure of success in areas where woodlots were unable to progress is indicative, on the other hand, of significant differences between them.

Diagnosis

Taking the common factors first, it is apparent that both the woodlots and the NFCP pursued a characteristically 'blueprint' style of approach. Objectives were determined without consulting the intended participants, and relatively inflexible technical packages were put together for dissemination. Unambiguous targets were laid down in advance, and it was expected that staff would adhere to them closely.

The discussion in Chapter 5 makes it clear that this was to prove wholly inappropriate in the case of the woodlots. To attempt to promote one or two pre-determined solutions in a range of diverse physical environments was, in itself, misguided. The error was then compounded by the expectation that, with the same minimal support, farmers would work to the same standard on sites requiring high labour inputs as they would on those in the most favoured locations.

These limitations were to become apparent from a comparatively early stage, and certain attempts were made to put things on a more satisfactory footing. The provision of tools and other assistance, under the WFP, has belatedly helped to

144

ease the difficulties of a few farmers through the initial period of high expenditures. The more active encouragement of inter-cropping and an expansion in the range of species made available also represent important steps towards a more farmer-centred approach; but all this has had to take place within a framework which retains fast-growing fuelwood species as its central feature.

Stoves present a less clear-cut situation, although it will be suggested that, here too, the fact that only one design was on offer was to act as a significant, if less obvious, constraint upon dissemination.

Shared misconceptions

The decision to operate in the blueprint mode, when other possibilities were, in principle, available, may initially be traced back to shared misconceptions about both the nature of biomass energy and the extent of the problem of its availability.

Biomass misunderstood
It was shown, in Chapter 2, how biomass was largely ignored in the first round of attempts to formulate energy policy in the 1970s and then subsequently colonized by commercial energy specialists as a part of the process by which the CEB was transformed into the MPE. Whilst formal recognition was eventually granted, in the documents produced at that time, to the central role that biomass performed, this was never reflected in any serious attempt to try to understand how the sector functioned. To the extent that it was examined at all, attention tended to focus on its capacity as a potential substitute for commercial energy, and, partly for this reason, the unique properties of biomass were never fully taken on board.

This was unfortunate, since earlier chapters have provided clear evidence that biomass differs fundamentally from other forms of energy. This is a function of the manner in which it is embedded in the contexts in which it is produced. It requires land to grow on, and is therefore subject to the range of independent factors which govern how, and by whom, that land should be used. It is generally not produced in its own right, but is grown as a by-product of other more highly valued commodities and is, therefore, subject to the forces which determine how these may be cultivated. It tends to be extracted and processed in labour time which is fitted in around, and hence conditioned by, the other work which the persons in question must perform.

Each of these supply-related factors may be highly location- and person-specific. The planners of the CFP, in particular, failed to recognize these peculiar characteristics of biomass. As a consequence, they treated it as if it were simply another homogeneous and readily compartmentalized branch of commercial energy production, which was amenable to 'command style' management, an assumption which dovetailed neatly with the forester's preference for centrally managed, plantation-type systems.

The problem overstated

Somewhat paradoxically, the second common misconception was to treat the fuelwood situation as being far more serious than it actually was. Both the numbers of people affected, and the wider implications which shortages were believed to have, became exaggerated.

A number of factors was responsible. As the account in Chapter 2 indicates, relatively little was actually known about how biomass energy was obtained and used at the time the major interventions were being designed. The few studies which were available were either not used, or were misinterpreted by policy-makers, whose perceptions were blinkered by their specialist interest in commercial energy. This created a vacuum into which ideas generated in international circles were able to flow largely unchallenged.

Already, caught largely unaware by rapid oil-price increases, and with growing concern about threats to the environment, those circles were, themselves, highly receptive to fears of fuelwood crisis. In this atmosphere, quite valid points about the energy problems of certain groups came to be treated as if they were general to all poor people. And since most poor people lived in rural areas, it seemed to follow logically that fuel shortage was primarily a rural problem. Biomass energy was also seen as a woman's issue, at a time when questions of gender were receiving increasing emphasis.[3] This all added up to a somewhat heady cocktail for international agencies. The FAO study, identifying Sri Lanka as a deficit country, provided the final confirmation that was required.[4]

If Sri Lankan policy-makers had their doubts about what was going on, they kept them to themselves. The international resources which were becoming available in the wake of the diagnosis would have been welcome, irrespective of the accuracy of the assumptions upon which it was based. This was particularly so in the case of the FD, which saw in the CFP a device which might, to a limited extent, assist in arresting the long-term deterioration in its fortunes. Even if the project were to come to nothing, jobs and opportunities for international training would have been created, additional vehicles made available, and much-needed housing provided for staff.

Even when allowance is made for these advantages, however, alarm bells ought to have started ringing, as more information began to become available through the early 1980s. Wijesinghe's study, conducted in 1983 and published in 1984, did not directly make the point itself, but carried the implicit message that rural people had a number of biomass energy options open to them. It also followed clearly from what Wijesinghe was saying that there could be little link between fuel consumption and deforestation.

By this stage, however, official perceptions of the problem were entrenched, to an extent which actually made it possible for Munasinghe to cite Wijesinghe quite extensively, whilst remaining, to all practical intents and purposes, oblivious to what was implied by the analysis. The stoves initiatives thus proceeded largely as they would otherwise have done. The same applied to the CFP, which was, by that stage, already under way.

The more detailed evidence provided by the FMP, some two years later, reinforced Wijesinghe. By this time, however, even more resources had been committed. Partly for this reason, and partly because fuel was no more than a minor element amongst more pressing concerns dealt with by the Plan, the message for biomass intervention was again not taken on board.

The FAO-inspired view of generalized fuelwood shortage thus continued to hold sway, sustaining a sense of urgency, and justifying the retention of command-style solutions. This, in turn, led on to a series of difficulties in the implementation stage.

147

Common difficulties

Geographical imbalances

In the first place, a quite serious mismatch arose between the geographical distribution of activities, and the actual locations of fuel shortages. Table 7.2 illustrates the extent of the disparity. It shows five districts in overall fuelwood deficit, but of these, only Kandy, Gampaha and Nuwara Eliya had

Table 7.2: Districts fuel balances and intervention priorities

District	Fuel balance tonnes[1] (thousands)	Stove programme priority ranking[2]	Forestry programme priority ranking[3]
Colombo	−373		
Kandy	−333	4	3
Gampaha	−228	7	
Nuwara Eliya	−176	8	3
Badulla	− 90		1
Matale	4	9	3
Matara	71	6	
Galle	77		
Jaffna	81		
Hambantota	111	3	
Batticaloa	123		2
Kalutara	178	10	
Ratnapura	270	2	
Kegalle	403	5	
Trincomalee	513		
Mannar	570		
Vavuniya	578		
Amparai	591		
Puttalam	640		
Kurunegala	774	1	
Polonnaruwa	808		
Anuradhapura	809		
Mullaitivu	853		
Monaragala	1110		

1. This is the overall biomass fuel balance as defined in Table 3.2. Districts are listed with the largest deficit at the top and the largest surplus at the bottom.
2. This refers to the situation in the first phase of the programme, the district with the largest number of stoves ranked number 1. A blank indicates no stoves. The urban programme, focused initially on Colombo and Gampaha, did not start until 1987, and is therefore not included.
3. Priority is based upon the total areas earmarked for planting in the initial project document, and includes block fuelwood plantations, as well as farmers' woodlots.

stove programmes under the NFCP, and only Kandy, Nuwara Eliya and Badulla featured in the CFP list. Turning to the 19 fuel-surplus districts, on the other hand, Table 7.2 indicates that seven had stoves programmes, and that two provided CFP sites.

If one delves a little further, even more surprising discoveries are made. In the case of stoves, the greatest individual concentration appears in Kurunegala which, by virtue of its coconut plantations and relatively low population densities, actually has the fifth largest fuel surplus of the country's 25 districts. Ratnapura and Hambantota, the districts with the next largest concentrations, also appear in the overall surplus category. In total, no less than 78 per cent of all stoves were installed in districts falling within the surplus group.

Colombo, on the other hand, with the largest concentrations of population, did not feature at all up until 1987, and neighbouring Gampaha, with the second highest densities, received only a relatively small allocation. These are the districts where most poor people have to buy fuel, and where it is most likely that fuel will, in future, be supplied in ways which contribute to deforestation.

As far as community forestry is concerned, distribution corresponded rather more closely to need, although anomalies are once again apparent. The initial prominence given to Batticaloa seems difficult to justify on any grounds. Similarly, it is hard to see why Badulla was chosen as the major centre, since its own deficit is quite small by comparison with other districts, and it is remote from the major centres of demand.

Taking the two interventions together, it is difficult to avoid the conclusion that both were project, rather than needs driven. With forestry, disproportionate attention appears to have been given to the availability of sites suitable for the growing of trees, to the exclusion of any consideration of what they might actually be used for when mature. With stoves, the main problems appear to derive from the fragmentation of decision-making and financial provision between donors, each of whom was linked to, and hence only able to act in, particular districts. A needs-centred approach would also necessarily have looked at the likely effect of the interventions in relation to one another, cutting back on one type of activity, where it appeared that

149

the other provided a more cost-effective means to a commonly desired end.

Problems of targeting groups

This impression of events being project driven is strengthened when one moves from the geographical spread of activities to consider distribution from the economic and social points of view. Evidence presented in Chapter 4 suggests that, even in overall deficit areas like Kandy and Badulla, it is only a small proportion of households which are placed in difficulty and that, far more often than not, it is the poorest who are adversely affected. Ideally, therefore, interventions should have been targeted on this group, but analysis in Chapters 5 and 6 indicates that this was not normally what happened.

Whilst it was found that some stoves were being adopted by the poorer households, which were most in need, the proportion of better-off households adopting was greater. In the case of woodlots, the disparity was even more pronounced, with hardly any poorer households able to participate successfully at all. Further evidence indicated that the project might even have had the effect of denying poor households, and especially poor women, access to their traditional sources of fuel.

The sense that fuel problems were general, the perceived need for rapid action, and the tendency for human considerations to become obscured behind physical output targets, all conspired to obscure the existence of differentiated need.

In the case of the woodlots, this oversight was then compounded by the additional failure to distinguish clearly between the intended end-users of the fuel to be produced. Certain references suggested that these were supposed to be rural people themselves, whilst others indicated that the primary purpose was to supply urban markets.

Users' priorities unacknowledged

If better information had been available, if better use had been made of what was already known, and if decision-makers had been more sensitively attuned to the properties of biomass as a fuel, then outcomes would clearly have been more successful than they were. However, whilst the satisfaction of these conditions would have helped to adapt interventions more efficiently to fuel needs, it would not

150

have been sufficient to have guaranteed a positive response from rural people.

This was particularly true with regard to woodlots. Wider issues about optimal land use, and competing end uses of tree products, were to exercise a significant influence upon the course of events, sometimes openly subverting project intentions, and sometimes creating the initial appearance of success, whilst storing up problems for the future. It was, above all else, this failure to take on board the wider set of needs influencing the resource-utilization decisions of rural people that explains the difficulties which were encountered.

Contrasting features

Having considered what the interventions held in common, we may now turn to the factors which distinguish them.

The technologies compared
Stoves have a number of distinctive characteristics:

o they are relatively inexpensive;
o benefits may be enjoyed from the time adoption has taken place;
o benefits can be appropriated by the user with little fear of interference from any external source;
o in cases where fuel is purchased, the pay-back period on the initial investment amounts to only a few months;
o the houses in which stoves are installed may be divided into a relatively small number of types, which means that once user preferences have been identified, the design process may proceed in a relatively centralized fashion within particular localities.

Woodlots, by contrast:

o entail heavy initial costs;
o are dependent upon the vagaries of climate;
o require co-operation, and the honouring of mutual rights and obligations between considerable numbers of households;
o have a pay-back period of at least seven years;
o require greater adaptation to individual circumstances,

151

and thus a higher degree of adopter participation and expertise.

The innovation process

Arriving at the right technical package with stoves may, in most respects, be just as complex in its own way as devising a workable set of forestry or agro-forestry practices. Once this point has been reached, however, the subsequent process of implementation becomes a relatively straightforward matter. The more important distinction between the two interventions lie, however, precisely in the nature of the respective innovation processes themselves.

Leaving aside the initial error of seeking to popularize the Lorena, the stove case was characterized by close interaction between designers and the rural women who were its prospective users. It was recognized, at an early stage, that fuel economy was not the only, and often not even the major, determinant of the individual adoption decisions upon which mass dissemination would ultimately depend. Care was, therefore, taken to produce a stove which, in terms of ease and flexibility of use, reproduced a high proportion of the characteristics which were valued in traditional designs. Attempts to eliminate smoke altogether were abandoned when it was realized that this could perform useful functions. Time was taken to get things right. Interaction was the order of the day.

Because the characteristics appealing to the individual user were already embodied in the design before the advent of the NFCP and the switch to the blueprint mode, and because these characteristics apparently transferred reasonably well to the new districts in which the stove was promoted, something approaching mass dissemination could be attained. The CFP, by contrast, was guilty of over-innovation, of trying to move too far and too quickly from pre-existing practices, and paid the inevitable price.

Towards a new biomass strategy

The broad principles derived from the first round of interventions provide clear indications as to how a biomass strategy might now be constructed, and how, in more general terms, the respective roles of government and rural people might be set upon a sounder footing.

152

Caveats

Before an alternative outline can be presented, it is important to recognize that the political situation in Sri Lanka has deteriorated markedly in the period since data were collected, making it almost impossible to predict when conditions might actually allow new ideas to be put into effect. It must, therefore, be made clear that everything which follows rests upon the assumption that confrontation will end, and that the earlier state of stability will be restored.

A second caveat should also be borne in mind. This is that it would clearly be inappropriate, in the light of what has been argued in the earlier part of this chapter, to attempt to advance an alternative strategy in blueprint form. A new approach could only succeed on the basis of a pooling of experience, and a process of negotiation between the various interested parties, including different groups of rural people, voluntary agencies, relevant parts of the government machinery, and aid donors. And even after an initial round of discussions, it would still be essential to proceed in a process mode.

As such, the discussion which follows represents no more than an attempt to outline what some of the key elements in that process might be, and to indicate some of the underlying principles by which it should be guided.

Distinguishing sectors

The first round of interventions was based upon the erroneous assumption that fuelwood scarcity was primarily a rural problem, whereas it is now apparent that the major focus should be upon the urban areas. It has also been noted, in passing, that industrial biomass consumption, whilst not very important in overall terms, may be of significance in particular areas of concentration.

Any strategy must start from a recognition of the distinctive nature and requirements of these sectors, as well as from an appreciation of the inter-relations, both current and potential, between them. Thinking back to the Kandy villages discussed in Chapter 3, for example, it will be recalled that the availability of fuel for domestic purposes had been influenced by the presence of the tobacco industry. It will also be recalled that there is the very real prospect of future commercial production to supply urban consumers, which may have implications for domestic availability.

Determining priorities

The second principle is that a clear sequence of priorities should be observed in reviewing possible courses of action. The first question to be asked, with regard to any sector, should be whether it is actually necessary to do anything at all. Often, as in the case of the majority of current rural fuel consumers, it may not be important for anyone to take action. Confronted with shortages, many consumers will be able to devise their own solutions, and apart from where this will entail some social cost, it will nearly always be better that they should be allowed to do so.

Under circumstances where it is established that some form of intervention will be required, the possibilities for conservation should be explored first. As the discussion in the previous section indicates, the Sri Lankan experience conforms to the general rule that this almost invariably proves more cost-effective than other forms of action. Only when this set of options has been exhausted may it be appropriate to turn to the generally much more complicated and expensive business of expanding supply.

The interaction between these two sets of priorities is set out in Table 7.3. In addition to the broad alternatives which have already been mentioned, the source of innovation axis incorporates an intermediate interactive category, to cover situations where insiders and outsiders work in collaboration.

When the three innovation styles are set against the consumption and supply possibilities, a six-box matrix results. Among the categories arising, pure insider conservation strategies rank highest, whilst pure outsider, supply-oriented options come lowest. The suggested principle is that 1-type options should be examined first, the second option only being entertained when the first have been shown to be inoperable, and so forth.

The discussion now moves on to consider how these principles, which govern priorities, intersect with those on the regional and social composition of need, which were explored earlier.

The rural sector

The rural sector will be dealt with first. Whilst not itself the area of primary need, it is the source from which almost all

Table 7.3: Ideal priorities for selecting responses to fuel shortage

Type of response	Improve conservation	Enhance supply
Insiders control innovation	1	2
Interactive innovation process	3	4
Outsiders control innovation	5	6

biomass fuel needs must ultimately be satisfied. As such, it provides a base from which the outlines of the industrial and urban dimensions of strategy may subsequently be sketched.

The account in Chapter 4 was built around communities in fuel-deficit districts, but suggested that, even here, there were no generalized fuel shortages. The only place where most households were neither largely self-sufficient in fuel, nor able to collect their requirements locally, was Nugathalawa and this mainly reflected the peri-urban character of the area. In the unequivocally rural settings of the other five communities, only a small proportion of households was found to incur significant costs in the course of satisfying their needs.

As far as the subsistence sector is concerned, there are therefore two problems to solve. The first is to enable those who are currently self-sufficient to maintain their position, if and when greater shortages begin to make themselves felt. The second is to improve the access enjoyed by those who currently face a certain degree of difficulty.

Rural people's role in energy conservation
Even if outsiders do nothing, certain responses to shortage are likely to occur. No attempt was made, in this research, to look in detail at the fuel-use practices of those for whom collection was most time consuming. Experience reported by others, however, suggests that it is likely that more economical fuel-use procedures will already have been introduced in

these instances, with a potential for savings of as much as 50 per cent, where other circumstances make the effort worthwhile.[5]

It appears highly likely that people with generally frugal lifestyles would already be aware of these options, and would not require any further instructions as to how to put them into effect, when individual circumstances made it sensible for them to do so. The potential savings achievable by the more sparing use of fuel actually exceed the average reduction in fuel consumption currently reported for the Sarvodaya stove, and seem the easiest of all to secure.

A second 'do nothing' scenario might entail rural people changing their own stove designs through a process of indigenous innovation, or imitation. The potential for this has already been shown to exist in a village near Hatton. This is an upland community where demand is high, supplies are short and villagers have themselves developed several different designs of stove.[6] A similar example is provided by the sawdust stove, used by certain households in Nugathalawa, which was described in Chapter 4. Those presently using the three-stone model could secure significant savings simply by installing an open-hearth.

Rural people's role in increasing fuel supply
No examples have been encountered of comparable insider fuel supply strategies, although it is quite possible that these exist. In other countries, where fuel shortages have already arisen to a greater extent, Leach and Mearns have shown how rural people are perfectly capable of such actions, not only in response to their own needs, but also as a part of the more complicated and risky business of producing to satisfy urban commercial demand.[7] Responses of this kind would only be open to the landed, but in rural Sri Lanka it is comparatively rare to find rural households with no home garden land at all.

Interactive routes to improved conservation
The next set of possibilities, conservation by interactive intervention, can be further sub-divided into minimalist and maximalist cases. The former might simply entail building a picture of the major characteristics of different indigenous stoves, and of the conditions under which they were used, and then making the necessary information known to

people in similar circumstances elsewhere, where innovations have not yet taken place.

Alternatively, a study might be conducted of the process of innovation in the Hatton village cited above, in order to arrive at principles which could then be employed in devising minimalist intervention strategies elsewhere. This would afford universities and research institutions an opportunity to become more directly involved in the policy-making process.

At the maximalist end of the spectrum, approaches could be devised along the lines of the original Sarvodaya intervention in Kandy, perhaps involving the offices of other voluntary organizations, or local-level government institutions.

Interactive supply measures
Parallel possibilities present themselves on the supply side. The excellent study by Jayanetti and Reddy[8] provides a sound basis for the understanding of the strategies pursued by Kandyan farmers in the management of their home gardens, to which work being undertaken by the NeoSynthesis Research Centre now promises to add a dynamic perspective. Such studies could be extended further to examine the role of fuelwood, and the findings then being made available to others in the same way as for stoves.

Maximalist possibilities here are illustrated in the participatory upland farming research currently being undertaken by IRDPs in Hambantota, Badulla and elsewhere. These properly focus on addressing overall farmer priorities, but can readily be modified, where necessary, to take fuel on board.

Building on the experience of Indonesia, and other countries, Shea has provided theoretical models for Sri Lanka which illustrate how this might be achieved.[9] A wide range of possibilities is indicated, some of which are suited to relatively good, and others to poorer soils. Some involve fruit trees, intercropped with minor export crops such as pepper, which may be trained up fuelwood-producing *Gliricidia*. Others have orchard trees intercropped with *Gliricidia*. Others still envisage rotations in which nitrogen-fixing fuelwood species feature periodically.

It is a striking feature of most of these options that they appear capable of generating as much fuelwood as the models originally promoted by the CFP, whilst simultaneously providing the other tree and non-tree products which farmers generally value more than fuel. The key to these possibilities is provided by the replacement of eucalyptus, which has to be in the ground for about seven years before it is harvested, with *Gliricidia*, which can be harvested after two years, and thus permits much greater flexibility in the design of land-use systems. Some of these possibilities are spelled out in more detail in Appendix 2, and are not dissimilar to ideas advanced by farmers themselves. This suggests that an interactive approach to further development would work well, and could quickly come up with appropriate solutions in many locations.

This covers point 4 in the set of possibilities provided in the matrix, and as far as the satisfaction of the rural subsistence fuel needs is concerned, it is possible that one would need to proceed no further.

The role of government

Option 5, the promotion of conservation by outsiders, is essentially what was attempted with stoves under the NFCP. This might be justified if the research outlined earlier pointed to the conclusion that individual designs were likely to have very wide applications. It is, however, likely that it would be better simply to support the widespread acquisition of the skills which would be required for local potters to make available a range of the best current indigenous designs to the consumers in their areas. This might be achieved through a process of potter-to-potter learning.

Option 6, supply-side options designed purely by outsiders, corresponds to the approach of the CFP, and would almost certainly not be resorted to under any circumstances. The most that might be required in practice would be for certain external skills to be fed into the process of plot design, perhaps by drawing upon the existing extensions expertise of the Minor Export Crop Department. In contrast to existing practice, nearly all research would be conducted on village land, taking into account the priorities and constraints in terms of which farmers must operate. Limited assistance in the provision of inputs, and initial financial support might also be appropriate.

In the cases of both conservation and of supply enhancement, the main responsibility of government would be to ensure that resources would be made available, first, in areas where shortages were most likely to be a problem, and within these, to try to ensure that households in need were given reasonable access. With stoves, in view of the widely reported reluctance of poor people to install a new design until they were in a position to make more wide-ranging kitchen improvements, it might be necessary to pay particular attention to the possibility of devices, such as the portable urban design, which could circumvent this problem. With home gardens, it might be possible to develop ideas with, and to impart skills to, landless people rather than working directly with land owners themselves. The landless could then provide land improvement and ongoing operational services for the landowners in exchange either for cash payments, or a share of the produce (which could include fuel).

This, and all other supply-oriented interventions, would be aimed at altering cultivation practices on individually owned and operated pieces of land. This would help to avoid many of the difficulties encountered by the CFP when public land was used.

Urban scenarios
It will be recalled, from Chapter 2, that administrative districts with high urban concentrations which are in fuel deficit are presently able to satisfy their requirements from the Mahaweli clearances and rubber replanting scheme. This means that fuel is, for the present, far cheaper than it is likely to be in a few years' time. Nobody can say exactly when increases will start to arise, and it now appears that the predicted downturn in rubber wood might be delayed rather longer than had initially been anticipated. Neverthless, it remains almost inevitable that real and accelerating price increases will start to be experienced within the present decade.

A 'do nothing' scenario
When this happens, the behaviour modifications already discussed under the rural 'do nothing' scenario may be expected to come into play again here. Most people, on the other hand, will lack the land resources from which to augment supply, and it will also be comparatively difficult for them to design new stoves for themselves. A greater degree of outsider involvement will therefore be required. The greater homogeneity of design requirements among

159

urban users, and their greater degree of integration with the market economy, both point towards the desirability of a more centralized and blueprint approach here.

A government role in conservation
This has already been recognized, and acted upon in the form of the joint CEB / ITDG initiative, which was discussed in the second part of Chapter 6. Ultimately, however, a point will be reached where supply enhancement will also be required. Even at this stage, however, a 'do nothing' scenario might initially suffice. Private traders are already organized to supply urban markets,[10] but currently do so only from fuel which arises as a by-product from land clearances. It is difficult to predict what will happen when these supplies start to run down, or how quickly a point might be reached at which farmers might actually be encouraged to go into fuel production on a commercial basis. As indicated earlier, the experience of other countries does, however, suggest that it is likely that such a point will be arrived at, and that a private-sector supply response will be forthcoming.

This should not be left to chance, however. Once some of the new production possibilities reviewed above have been field-tested, and basic input/output data become available, economic calculations should be carried out to determine the attractiveness and feasibility of farm-based fuel supply strategies in locations from which urban supply might be contemplated. These, in turn, should be accompanied by further studies which look at the feasibility of larger-scale charcoal production in more distant locations. Block fuelwood plantations, of the kind now being pursued by the CFP, might also be contemplated. The difficulties inherent in large-scale interventions on land where no clear private right of ownership existed would, however, mean that this option should be regarded very much as a last resort. Universities and research institutions could again be commissioned to conduct such studies.

Industrial scenarios

We turn, finally, to the question of what might be attempted in the biomass-consuming parts of the industrial sector. Two broad situations arise here: the land-based biomass users, comprising the tea, coconut, tobacco and rubber industries, which together account for about 60 per cent of all industrial biomass energy consumption; and the non-land based activities, which include hotels, bricks and tiles, and bakeries, which together account for most of the remaining 40 per cent.

The 'do nothing' scenario

As far as the former are concerned, there is the possibility of both conservation and supply options being pursued under a 'do nothing' scenario, and this, in general, is what has already happened. All major industries are already taking effective steps on the conservation side. With regard to supply, neither coconut nor rubber producers need do much, since their existing fuel output, in the form of by-products, already exceeds consumption requirements by a comfortable margin. With tea, on the other hand, an in-built deficit is already being counteracted by a systematic on-site fuelwood plantation programme, through which total self-sufficiency will be attained within a short period of time.

The problem of tobacco

Tobacco, which is not organized on a plantation basis, and where those who dominate the industry do not directly control either the land or the barns where processing takes place, presents a rather different set of problems. These can probably best be overcome in the long run by helping barn owners, who normally have access to land, to embark upon the process of establishing their own plantations, as already happens to a limited extent. As is the case with tea, fast-growing *Gliricidia*, which is adequate for domestic consumption, will not be sufficient here, and different strategies, built around slower-maturing species will have to be pursued.

Supplying other industries

The non-agriculturally based industries must also be internally sub-divided. The brick industry, like the tobacco industry, will require large trunks, but being concentrated in close proximity to major coconut-growing areas, the industry is likely to be able to satisfy most of its requirements from this source. Bakeries, on the other hand, are likely to depend upon rubber wood and to pay the higher prices which may be required. Hotels could rely on the same sources as domestic comsumers and the possibilities outlined in that discussion will, therefore, once again apply in this instance. Bakeries and hotels would also seem to be areas where the expertise of ITDG, which has so far been deployed mainly in relation to domestic consumers, might usefully be put to work, once the higher-priority domestic design isues have been successfully resolved.

Conclusion

A new role for government
The biomass strategy which has been outlined is altogether more fluid than the existing approaches which have been described in this book. Problems are less serious than was imagined in the early 1980s but, at the same time, far more differentiated by location and socio-economic group. Urban problems may, to some extent at least, require the type of blueprint approach originally taken up in relation to the rural areas, although, even here, markets can do much of the work which was previously taken on by the government itself.

As far as rural areas are concerned, there is no need to move quickly on a large scale, but there is a need for enquiries, and for processes of innovation, to be set in motion upon several fronts. The proper role of government, and of the donors whose influence in this area of decision-making is strong, will entail broadening, but at the same time making shallower the extent of their involvement. They should seek, in other words, to withdraw to some extent from their present operational role, and to concentrate more upon the strategic provision of the guidance and incentives which are required to bring other actors into play.

Energy and the environment
This argument must, however, be subject to one final qualification. In the late 1970s and early 1980s, when the ideas which helped to shape the programmes which have been discussed were in the process of formation, people were much concerned with linkages between fuel use and environmental degradation. It was commonly supposed that, by dealing with the first problem, it would be possible simultaneously to go a long way towards solving the other.

162

These linkages have now been shown to be largely imaginary, but the environmental problems remain real enough. Hopefully, this exercise has performed a useful function in making this clear, and in thus helping to clear the way for a more accurate analysis of the true causes of environmental degradation. It is also likely that the new forms of private land use which have been dicussed will have applications on the public land which needs, for environmental reasons, to be protected too.

A process approach will certainly have to be deployed if the necessary support of local communities is to be mobilized, which suggests another way in which the consideration of the narrow problem of fuel provision may help to throw light on wider questions of environmental protections, or rural resource management more generally. As Chapter 5 indicated, however, the process of extending activities to public land raises a host of institutional problems which do not arise elsewhere. As Leach and Mearns have argued in relation to Africa,[11] so too in Sri Lanka will people need increasingly, and with increasing urgency, to look beyond the woodfuel crisis to the wider set of issues which this poses.

Notes

1. See Casley and Lury (1982).
2. Munasinghe (1986).
3. See Agarwal (1986).
4. See FAO (1981).
5. See Foley and Moss (1985).
6. Bill Stewart, personal communication.
7. See Leach and Mearns (1988).
8. Jayanetti and Reddy.
9. Shea (1987).
10. See Howes (1986/8).
11. Leach and Mearns (1988).

Appendix 1.   Research methods

The research began in October 1986. The first three months were spent assembling and reviewing secondary sources of information, consulting relevant authorities and making preliminary visits to possible fieldwork locations.

With the initial phase completed, a team of four research assistants, who had all recently completed degrees in agriculture, were recruited in January 1987. The team then embarked on a seven-month period of fieldwork supported by periodic input from consultants with expertise in specific areas of concern.

Choice of location

Major field studies were conducted in the districts of Badulla, Hambantota and Kandy with approximately equal periods of time being spent in each. These were chosen, in the first instance, because they contained high concentrations of fuelwood-related project activity.

The town of Badulla accommodates the headquarters of the CFP, and the district provides examples of all of the main types of work which have been initiated under its auspices. Hambantota was selected mainly because, at that time, it had the largest number of new stoves introduced under the CEB programme.[1] Kandy, as the district in which the new stove had been designed and first disseminated, also had quite a large concentration; together with a number of community forestry sites.

A second important criterion was the likelihood of fuel shortages. Each of the three districts is 'fuelwood deficit' as defined in Chapter 3, and Kandy and Badulla both also fall within the more restrictive 'overall deficit' category. A final consideration was that, between them, the three districts offered a reasonably broad spectrum of environmental types, ranging from the Wet, through the Intermediate, to the Dry Zone.

Districts with high concentrations of project activity, but with little evidence of fuel shortage, such as Ratnapura, were excluded. Districts where there was an apparent need for action, but where no interventions had at that time taken place, such as Colombo and Gampaha, were also excluded. Batticaloa, as the only Dry Zone location of the CFP, and as a district where there is some evidence of shortages, would ideally have been included, but was ruled out by the security situation. The procedures for identifying research locations within the main study districts differed according to the subjects under investigation, and to local conditions.

In Kandy, four of the active community forestry sites clustered in adjoining hamlets around a central village, which thus provided a very convenient base for the initial investigation. The entire team was able to live in close proximity and to meet several times each week, making it easy to provide regular supervision of assistants as they gained experience.

As the initial period of fieldwork drew to a close, other community forestry sites and areas with heavy concentrations of new stoves, were then visited for a series of studies. Each of these lasted for between one and two days.

Community forestry sites in Badulla were more scattered, so a decision was taken to establish a central base in the district town itself, from which three groups, located in different directions some distance from the town, were then investigated in some depth for the duration of the study, with the main researcher and consultants making regular visits and occasionally staying overnight.

Apart from providing the centre for the CFP, the district is also an important focus of the fuelwood trade. This made it possible to carry out a series of further investigations linking Badulla itself, and the other major urban centre of Bandarawela, to their sources of supply to the north and to the east.

In Hambantota, interest focused on stove adoption, a series of small-scale forestry activities, and the organization of the more localized woodfuel trade. In view of the wide geographical spread of activities, and the difficulty of arranging accommodation outside the coastal town, it was decided, in this instance, to establish a base in the district town itself, and then to travel out to fieldwork locations each day.

Subjects investigated

The types of data collected may be divided initially into two broad categories. First, we looked at the interventions themselves. This entailed measuring inputs and outputs, establishing who enjoyed access and who was excluded, and exploring the implications for both adopters/participants, and for others not directly involved, in order to arrive at an overall assessment of performance. Second, we conducted a series of broader enquiries designed to explain why observed outcomes arose. A final set of investigations entailed the elucidation of farmers' own suggestions for land-use systems which would best satisfy their fuel and other requirements.

Methods

A range of data collection methods was employed in each location. Official sources, such as electoral registers and project records, were consulted, and utilized wherever practicable. On a few occasions, it was possible to draw directly upon the results of surveys already conducted by consultants, planners or other researchers. Direct observation also played its part, being used extensively in the initial stages of each field investigation to arrive at an understanding of broad land-use and settlement patterns, the cultivation practices associated with specific land types, and the types of fuel available and used.

Heaviest reliance was placed upon various kinds of interview technique. These included: extensive questionnaire-based sample surveys, more detailed questionnaire-based case studies, administered to smaller numbers of purposively selected informants, and semi-structured interviews of key informants, using check lists of questions.

Each major data collection exercise was followed by a period of analysis and discussion, from which preliminary conclusions were derived. Ideas would then be tested in seminars organized for locally based implementation agencies.

The range of subjects investigated and the methods utilized differed to some extent from one place to another, but the following major elements were generally included.

A preliminary census, covering all households within the

166

chosen communities who were participating in the central activity under investigation, together with an equivalent number of non-participants. This provided data from which individual households could be classified into economic categories, together with basic information about energy consumption. (A slightly modified version was administered in studies of stove adoption, to allow for the fact that no other survey work was generally carried out in places where this was investigated.)

A questionnaire survey about project performance, administered to a randomly selected sample of project participants, comprising either 25 or 50 per cent of the entire population according to group size. This would generally be reinforced by a series of key informant interviews.

A questionnaire survey, concerning the major recent economic and social changes encountered by project participants and non-participants, with informants being purposively selected to represent the rich, middle and poor economic strata in each location. These were complemented by a series of key informant interviews, which were used to identify major changes affecting communities as a whole over a longer timespan.

Case studies dealing with contemporary household production and consumption behaviour,with informants selected also to represent the rich, middle and poor economic strata in each location. These would often be administered alongside detailed enquiries into the management of home garden and other upland plots.

Case studies exploring farmers' own preferences regarding agro-forestry practices, with informants initially being selected from different strata, but with the most interesting ideas then being explored in greater depth, irrespective of their origin.

Case studies dealing with domestic fuel production, consumption and use, with informants again selected to represent different strata.

In communities where interventions were not investigated in depth, only the key informant method was normally used.

Notes

1. Kurunegala has now most probably overtaken it.

167

Appendix 2. Potential fuel-producing agro-forestry systems designed by the consultant to the CFP

Figure 8.1: *The conversion of an area of shifting cultivation to minor export crops*

Year 1	Year 2	Year 3
Cultivated and *Gliricidia* planted	Minor export crop planted under *Gliricidia*	*Gliricidia* + minor export crop
Unused	Cultivated and *Gliricidia* planted	Minor export crop planted under *Gliricidia*
Unused	Unused	Cultivated and *Gliricidia* planted
Unused	Unused	Unused
Unused	Unused	Unused

Year 4	Year 5	Year 6
Gliricidia + minor export crop	*Gliricidia* + minor export crop	*Gliricidia* + minor export crop
Gliricidia + minor export crop	*Gliricidia* + minor export crop	*Gliricidia* + minor export crop
Minor export crop planted under *Gliricidia*	*Gliricidia* + minor export crop	*Gliricidia* + minor export crop
Cultivated and *Gliricidia* planted	Minor export crop planted under *Gliricidia*	*Gliricidia* + minor export crop
Unused	Cultivated and *Gliricidia* planted	Minor export crop planted under *Gliricidia*

Figure 8.2: *Conversion of an area of shifting cultivation to fruit orchard with inter-cropped nitrogen-fixing fuelwood trees*

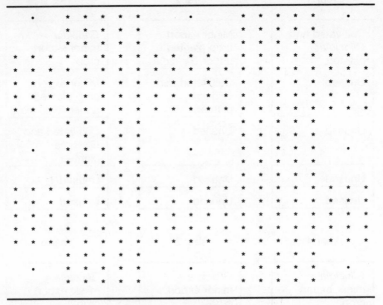

Key:

. *Fruit tree – 10m × 10m spacing, or 100 trees a hectare*

* *Fuelwood tree – 1m apart in rows, or 7500 trees a hectare*

Bibliography

Agarwal, B. (1986), *Cold hearths and barren slopes. The woodfuel crisis in the Third World*, Zed Press.

Amarasekera, R.M. (1986), *National fuelwood conservation programme of Sri Lanka*, Ceylon Electricity Board.

Amarasekara, R. M. and B.P. Sepalage, (1988), 'Sri Lankan stoves past and present' in *Boiling Point* No. 15, Intermediate Technology Development Group.

Asian Development Bank (1982), *Appraisal of the community Forestry Project in the Democratic Socialist Republic of Sri Lanka*, Manila.

Asian Development Bank (1987), *Community Forestry Project mid-term review*, Manila.

Casley, D.J. and D.A. Lury (1982), *Monitoring and evaluation of agriculture and rural development projects*, World Bank.

Clarke, K. (1990), 'Marketing Strategy to Disseminate Improved Stoves Throughout Sri Lanka', Intermediate Technology Development Group.

Department of Census and Statistics (1983), *Labour force and socio-economic survey 1980/1. Household income and expenditure*, Colombo.

Eckholm, E.P. (1975), *The other energy crisis*, World Watch Paper No.1, World Watch Institute.

Eckholm, E. P. (1976), *Losing ground*, Pergamon Press.

FAO (1981), *Map of the fuelwood situation in the developing countries: explanatory note*.

Farmer, B.H. (1954), 'Problems of land use in the dry zone of Ceylon', *The Geographical Journal*, Vol. cxx, Part I.

Foundation for Woodstove Dissemination (1987), 'Stoves for people, statement of the meeting', *International Workshop*, Guatemala.

Foley, G. and G. Barnard, (1984), 'Farm and community forestry', Earthscan Energy Information Programme', Technical Report No.3.

P.Moss (1985), 'Improved cooking stoves in developing countries', Earthscan Energy Information Programme, Technical Report No.2.

Gamage, D. (1987), *Community Forestry Project baseline survey*, Agrarian Research and Training Institute, Colombo.

Greeley, M. (1989), *Energy, agriculture and poverty: a review of issues and two case studies of renewable energy technologies in Sri Lanka*, Institute of Development Studies.

Howes, M. *et al.* (1983), 'The Sarvodaya Stoves Project: a critical review of developments 1979–82', Intermediate Technology Development Group, Stoves Project Report No.3.6

Howes, M. (1988a), 'The socio-economic context of fuel production and use in selected rural communities', Biomass Energy Research Project, Work in Progress Paper No.6, Institute of Development Studies.

Howes, M. (1988b), 'The Hambantota Stoves Project', *Boiling Point*, No.15, Intermediate Technology Development Group.

Howes, M. (1988c), 'A Preliminary Assessment of the Community Forestry Project', Biomass Energy Research Project, Work in Progress Paper No.7, Institute of Development Studies.

Howes, M. (1989), 'Identifying biomass fuel shortages in Sri Lanka', *Biomass* 26, Vol.19.

Jayanetti, E. and V.B. Reddy, (nd), 'The economic structure of Kandyan forest-garden farms', UNDP/FAO Agricultural Diversification Project, Department of Export Crops.

Jones, M. (1989), 'Sri Lanka bilateral woodburning stoves project. Internal Evaluations', Ceylon Electricity Board and Intermediate Technology Development Group.

Joseph, S. (1983), *A preliminary evaluation of the impact of woodburning stove programmes*, Food and Agriculture Organization.

Krugmann, H. (1987), *Review of issues and research relating to improved cookstoves*, International Development Research Centre.

Leach, G. (1984), *Household energy use and prices: Bangladesh, India, Pakistan and Sri Lanka*, International Institute for Environment and Development, London.

Leach, G. and R. Mearns (1988), *Beyond the woodfuel crisis*, Earthscan.

Liyange, C. (1986), 'National Fuelwood Conservation Programme', *Boiling Point*, No.16, Intermediate Technology Development Group.

Manibog, F.R. (1984), 'Improved cooking stoves in developing countries: problems and opportunities', *Annual Review of Energy*, Vol. 9.

Ministry of Finance and Planning (1984), *National Agriculture. Food and Nutrition Strategy*, Colombo.

Ministry of Lands and Land Development (1986), *Forestry master plan for Sri Lanka*, Colombo.

Ministry of Mahaweli Development (1985), *Mahaweli projects and programme*.

Ministry of Plan Implementation (1983), *Socio-economic Indicators of Sri Lanka*.

Ministry of Power and Energy (1985), *A biomass strategy for Sri Lanka*, Colombo.

Munasinghe, M. (1986), *Integrated national energy planning and management: methodology and applications in Sri Lanka*, World Bank, Washington DC.

National Science Council of Sri Lanka (1982), *Compendium of research and development projects in Sri Lanka on energy-related problems 1981*.

Rowcliffe, P. (1988), *The performance and potential of projects to design and disseminate improved wood-burning stoves in Asia*, MA dissertation, University of East Anglia.

Sankar, T. (1978), *Towards an Energy Policy for Sri Lanka*.

Shea, G.A. (1987), 'Community forestry consultant's report. Part I. Comments on mid-term review report for Community Forestry Project', Forestry Department.

Smith, K.R. (1987), 'Cookstove smoke and health', in *Boiling Point*, No.13, Intermediate Technology Development Group.

Statistics Department, Central Bank of Ceylon (1985a), 'Report on consumer finances and socio-economic survey 1981/2 Part II', Colombo.

Statistics Department, Central Bank of Ceylon (1985b), 'Price and wages statistics 1984', Colombo.

Sumanasekera, H.D. (1986), 'Evaluation of the fuelwood efficient stoves project', Hambantota Integrated Rural Development Project.

UNDP/World Bank Energy Sector Asssessment Program (1982), *Sri Lanka: issues and options in the energy sector.*

Van der Knyff, T. 'Netherlands–Sri Lanka energy programmes', *Boiling Point*, No.15, Intermediate Technology Development Group.

Wijesinghe, L.C.A. de S. (1984), 'A sample study of fuel consumption in Sri Lanka households', *Biomass*, Vol. 5.

Some other useful books from Intermediate Technology Publications

Energy Options: An introduction to small-scale renewable energy technologies
Edited and introduced by Drummond Hislop
Renewable energy can present a baffling array of options to aid agency managers, government officials, and advisers. This publication contrasts the relative merits of biomass, solar, hydro, and wind power, as well as detailing some direct applications.
112pp, ISBN 1 85339 082 8

The Power Guide: An international catalogue of small-scale energy equipment
With introductions by Wim Hulscher and Peter Fraenkel
Dealing with renewable energy sources (wind, sun, water, and biomass), this book catalogues small-scale energy equipment (up to 250kW) and provides information on hundreds of products from around 500 manufacturers and suppliers in over 40 countries.
296pp, ISBN 1 85339 192 1

Improved Wood Waste and Charcoal Burning Stoves: A practitioner's manual
W. Stewart and others
A manual for those involved in the day-to-day work of stoves projects. The book describes the chief characteristics, both advantages and disadvantages, of 28 types of stoves.
240pp, ISBN 0 946688 65 6

INTERMEDIATE TECHNOLOGY PUBLICATIONS

103–105 SOUTHAMPTON ROW   LONDON WC1B 4HH   UK